"Shirley has given us yet another important reason to understand our own personality and our greatest needs."

— FLORENCE LITTAUER, popular speaker and best-selling author of *Personality Plus; Silver Boxes; Making the Blue Plate Special*

"I admired Shirley the first time I met her, but after reading her insightful book, I admire her so much more for having the courage to point out her weaknesses. In doing so, she gave me permission to examine my own. By admitting our weaknesses, we give others the strength to do it, too. I want to cry for her for being so brave."

— DIANE HEAVIN CREDENTIALS, co-founder, Curves International; publisher, *Diane Magazine*

THE
EVE
FACTOR

SHIRLEY ROSE

NAVPRESS®

BRINGING TRUTH TO LIFE

OUR GUARANTEE TO YOU

We believe so strongly in the message of our books that we are making this quality guarantee to you. If for any reason you are disappointed with the content of this book, return the title page to us with your name and address and we will refund to you the list price of the book. To help us serve you better, please briefly describe why you were disappointed. Mail your refund request to: NavPress, P.O. Box 35002, Colorado Springs, CO 80935.

The Navigators is an international Christian organization. Our mission is to reach, disciple, and equip people to know Christ and to make Him known through successive generations. We envision multitudes of diverse people in the United States and every other nation who have a passionate love for Christ, live a lifestyle of sharing Christ's love, and multiply spiritual laborers among those without Christ.

NavPress is the publishing ministry of The Navigators. NavPress publications help believers learn biblical truth and apply what they learn to their lives and ministries. Our mission is to stimulate spiritual formation among our readers.

ISBN 1-57683-818-8

Cover Design: The DesignWorks Group
Cover Photo: Steve Gardner, Pixelworks Studios
Creative Team: Terry Behimer, Liz Heaney, Darla Hightower, Arvid Wallen, Pat Reinheimer, Bob Bubnis

Some of the anecdotal illustrations in this book are true to life and are included with the permission of the persons involved. All other illustrations are composites of real situations, and any resemblance to people living or dead is coincidental.

Unless otherwise identified, all Scripture quotations in this publication are taken from the HOLY BIBLE: NEW INTERNATIONAL VERSION® (NIV®). Copyright © 1973, 1978, 1984 by International Bible Society. Used by permission of Zondervan Publishing House. All rights reserved. Other versions used include: the *Revised Standard Version Bible* (RSV), copyright 1946, 1952, 1971, by the Division of Christian Education of the National Council of the Churches of Christ in the USA, used by permission, all rights reserved; *The Living Bible* (TLB), Copyright © 1971, used by permission of Tyndale House Publishers, Inc., Wheaton, IL 60189, all rights reserved; the *Holy Bible, New Living Translation* (NLT), copyright © 1996. Used by permission of Tyndale House Publishers, Inc., Wheaton, Illinois 60189, all rights reserved; and the *King James Version* (KJV).

Rose, Shirley, 1947-

    The Eve factor : resisting and overcoming temptation / Shirley Rose.
        p. cm.
    Includes bibliographical references.
    ISBN 1-57683-818-8
    1. Christian women--Religious life. 2. Temptation. I. Title.
    BV4527.R665 2006
    248.8'43--dc22

                            2005037413

Published in Association with the literary agency of Les H. Stobbe, 300 Doubleday Road, Tryon, NC 28782.

Printed in the United States of America

1 2 3 4 5 6 / 10 09 08 07 06

FOR A FREE CATALOG OF NAVPRESS BOOKS & BIBLE STUDIES,
CALL 1-800-366-7788 (USA) OR 1-800-839-4769 (CANADA)

CONTENTS

ACKNOWLEDGMENTS

To my husband Jerry: Your encouragement and interest in my work and ministry mean so much. You are the busiest person I know, yet you took the time to read each chapter. Your contribution to this book was profound. Your friendship is precious. Your love is my anchor. This book was written for women, but you got it! Thanks.

Most of the women's names in this book have been changed to protect their privacy. I wish to thank all the women who have shared their stories on my television program *Aspiring Women* and with me personally. Your honesty and courage to share about your struggles with temptation motivated and enabled me to write this book. Without you it would not have been possible. I am deeply grateful.

IT'S NOT ALWAYS ABOUT SEX

Understanding the Subtleties of Temptation

Now the works of the flesh are not only adultery,
fornication, and sexual fantasies,
but also include hatred, creating strife, jealousy,
outbursts of anger, selfish ambition,
complaining, criticizing, and envy.

GALATIANS 5:19-21 (AUTHOR'S PARAPHRASE)

For the last ten years I have been the executive producer and cohost of a women's television program called *Aspiring Women*. God has used this show to touch women in significant ways throughout the United States and in more than thirty countries. I have two extremely gifted and beautiful cohosts, Michelle McKinney Hammond and Tammy Maltby, who appear on the show with me. We are good friends and I have great affection and respect for them. Although we work hard, the three of us always have a wonderful time when we get together.

A few years ago, however, I noticed an unpleasant change in me whenever Tammy and Michelle came in to do the shows. Although I enjoyed their company and talking about what was happening in our lives, my heart was heavy. The television programs were going well, but I felt sad and lacked a sense of peace. It was as if I were in the midst of a wonderful party, surrounded by good friends, great food and music, but having a miserable time and wanting to go home. I found myself getting irritated and agitated for no reason. Even though I felt sure I was doing what God wanted me to do, I no longer experienced the joy and satisfaction I once had.

When Michelle and Tammy would talk about all the amazing opportunities God was giving them, I felt I had little to contribute to those conversations. Afterward, I would have a chat with God that went something like this: *God, I love Tammy and Michelle. I am so happy for all the great things that are happening in their lives. But what about me? They seem so much more talented, beautiful, and articulate than I am. None of those exciting things are happening in my life.*

Though we remained friends, I found myself thinking negative thoughts about my cohosts. I stopped short of gossip, but inwardly I became critical of them. In my mind I magnified any small mistake they made. Though all three of us are outgoing and talkative, their constant chatter sometimes got on my nerves. I became less tolerant of their idiosyncrasies and became annoyed with them, finding fault unnecessarily.

I finally became so concerned I asked the Lord to show me why I was feeling this way. To my great surprise and dismay, God showed me I was *jealous* of Tammy and Michelle! Me — jealous! I couldn't have been more shocked. How could that possibly be? After all, I hate jealousy. I have seen it tear families apart, ruin relationships, and do irreparable harm. How could I have allowed this sin to sneak into my heart, steal my joy, and threaten to destroy not only my relationships with these two women, but also our television ministry?

I am thankful God slowly began to reveal the answers to these questions. I'll go into more detail about this later in the book, but for now let me say that my jealousy came from having given in to the temptation of inappropriate comparisons.

If I had realized that I was being tempted and had refused to make these comparisons, the temptation would not have turned into jealousy. And if I had not recognized this sin in my life and dealt with it, I don't think the television program would have continued.

Many Christian women have similar struggles. This was confirmed to me when I did a show on temptation. My husband Jerry was out of town, and I asked a woman to join me in hosting our live, one-hour call-in program. At the top of the show I talked briefly about my problem with jealousy, and then we asked women to anonymously call in their secret temptations. The response was amazing. Our phones were jammed. We had never received more calls. One woman after another called, and on live television, admitted to struggling with jealousy, resentment, bitterness, unforgiveness, feelings of rejection, anger, and other sins.

I've heard similar stories from hundreds of women around the world. Like me, many of them were not aware they were giving in to temptation and engaging in sinful behaviors and patterns that were robbing them of peace and joy. I think one reason for this is when most of us think about temptation, we immediately think about *sexual* temptation. And for good reason. Sexual immorality is rampant in our postmodern society, and it affects women as well as men. The allure of sexual sin must be taken seriously. However, it's not always about sex. Most women struggle with other temptations on a more regular basis. Left unchecked, these areas of temptation can lead to serious sins of the spirit. I propose there are *other* temptations women face in the day-to-day business of living that are just as lethal to a close, fulfilling relationship with God and a fruitful ministry.

The very first woman gave in to the enticement of temptation, and women have been following in her footsteps ever after. Like Eve, we can be duped into believing that we'll gain something rewarding if we act out on the temptation. All of us are susceptible. All of us have The Eve Factor.

THE EVE FACTOR

Why did Eve eat that apple when God had specifically said not to do so? "But you must not eat from the tree of the knowledge of good and evil" (Genesis 2:17). We know she couldn't have been hungry. After all, Eve lived in a beautiful garden with an abundance of delicious food. The climate was perfect, the scenery breathtaking. There were no dangers, no stress. She had a gorgeous husband, and they were still on their honeymoon. She had no clothes to wash, in fact, no clothes at all. No housework to do, no children to care for. Best of all, Adam and Eve had no guilt or regrets. They had a close, intimate relationship with God, and He came and visited them every day. It was truly paradise. What more could Eve possibly want? Why did she do the one thing she was commanded not to do?

Eve sinned because she bought into the lie behind the temptation. Satan told her if she ate the apple she would be like God (see Genesis 3:5)—and so she ate the forbidden fruit. However, she did *not* become like God. Instead her fellowship with Him was broken, and for the first time she experienced the heartbreak of guilt and shame. Satan enticed her with the promise that she could rise above her present position. It wasn't true. The serpent also told her she would not die, but the moment she disobeyed God, she was doomed to die.

By casting doubt on what God had said, Satan encouraged Eve to justify her actions. And by enticing her with something she wanted—wisdom and significance—he persuaded Eve to disobey God's command. Eve yielded to the temptations of *pride, selfish ambition,* and *dissatisfaction,* and the fallout was catastrophic. Eve not only made a sinful choice herself, she convinced Adam to do likewise. They both died spiritually and got kicked out of paradise. Their failure introduced sin and its devastation into a perfect world. We are still listening to temptation's lies today.

So what is The Eve Factor? The Eve Factor is the propensity to believe the lies of the Enemy, rationalize our behavior, make a decision to do what is against God's rules, and then bring others into sin with us.

THE SUBTLE TEMPTATIONS WOMEN FACE

Often the temptations women face are not as obvious as Eve's. We may not even realize we are compromising our standards or making a decision to do what is wrong. We rarely cause others to sin intentionally. But most of us are confronted with The Eve Factor daily.

Here are some examples of the kinds of subtle temptations women face:

Complacency. Some women succumb to temptation, not by what they *do* but by what they *fail* to do. For instance, some women would rather remain in a bad situation than to take the risk of facing the unknown. They stay in abusive or unhappy relationships because they are not willing to do what it takes to make things better. They believe the lie that their husband (or boyfriend) will change. Others stay in destructive relationships so they can play the victim and excuse their own part in the problem, putting themselves and their children in danger.

A few years ago I interviewed Jennifer O'Neill, a former superstar model and actress. When I was a young person I thought Jennifer was the most beautiful woman I'd ever seen. I wanted to be a movie star like her. I was shocked when Jennifer told me that although she had become an international model at sixteen years of age and a successful actress, she always felt ugly and had poor self-esteem.

She worked hard to please people and gain acceptance at any cost, especially the acceptance of men, and went through several unsuccessful marriages. She said, "If you have low self-esteem, you don't invite people who treat you well into your life, because you don't have a good sense of yourself."

One of Jennifer's husbands sexually abused her fourteen-year-old daughter. The daughter tried to tell her, but Jennifer said that her husband was a good liar and she chose to believe him rather than her daughter. (The courts didn't believe the daughter's story either.) Her poor self-esteem made her cling to this relationship and others that followed to the point that she couldn't see the truth. The unhealthy dependency of her relationship resulted in complacency as a parent. She should have seen what was happening and taken action to protect her daughter. (By the way, the guy molested his next stepdaughter and eventually landed in prison.)

Overspending and overeating. Some are tempted to spend too much money on things they don't need because they are trying to ease the pain and fill an emptiness they can't quite identify. Other women do the same thing with food.

Doing too much. There are those who just can't seem to say "no." Do you realize that the need to please people and overextend yourself is a snare of the Enemy? Many of us succumb to the dangerous temptation to let our lives get out of balance.

Nancy was a busy, happy wife who said "yes" to everything. She describes herself as a high-strung perfectionist who could juggle a lot of tasks. It gave her a feeling of power, accomplishment, and acceptance. However, when she had a baby and had to relocate her family soon afterward, the stress intensified. A death in the family put her over the edge. She began to have anxiety and panic attacks that resulted in her hospitalization and a major breakdown. It took months of therapy and a lifestyle change to bring healing.

Negative thinking, fear, and worry. Other women approach life from a negative point of view. They allow worrying, worst-case scenarios, and fear to dominate their lives and rob them of the joy and peace God intended for His children.

Conforming to the world's values. Some of us find it difficult to live a righteous life in an ungodly society. We are tempted to dress as provocatively as the world, spend our money the same way, put too much emphasis on things, and even divorce our husbands for no good reason. Instead of being lights in the world, we are influenced by those around us.

Creating strife and contention. Strong-willed, aggressive women can create contention and strife wherever they go. The Enemy makes us believe we have all the answers, that our way is best, and that others should do our bidding.

I recently counseled Debbie, a precious mother of three teenagers. She is a generous, loving woman who works tirelessly in her church. But she confided that she struggles with anger, yelling, and bullying her husband and children. She knows this is wrong and that she is making her family miserable, but she can't seem to stop. The fallout of this destructive habit is not only a chaotic home but loads of guilt and limited spiritual growth. She loves God and wants to be a good mother, but she continually feels like a failure.

Many of us see these destructive patterns in our lives but allow them to continue year after year. We want lives of purpose that please God, but we yield to subtle temptations that hold us back. How do we get ourselves into such a predicament?

Understanding Temptation

To answer this question, we need to understand what temptation is and how it works. This common definition is in line with the biblical definition of temptation:

that which attempts to persuade or entice one to do something wrong or unwise by the prospect of pleasure or advantage.[1]

It Offers Us Something We Want

The word *temptation* implies that something is being dangled in front of a person in order to entice or persuade her to do something God says is wrong. This is certainly how some people were tempted in the Bible. We've already looked at how Satan enticed Eve; he also tempted Christ three different times in the wilderness by dangling something that would have given Christ relief or pleasure — for the moment. Esau tempted Jacob to give up his birthright by offering him a bowl of stew when he was famished, and Potiphar's wife enticed Joseph with the promise of sexual pleasure.

It Is Oh So Subtle

To help you understand the subtle nature of temptation, I want you to picture this fictional scenario.

Sarah and Jim have been married for over fifteen years. The marriage hasn't been perfect; they've had some issues. But Sarah has never even considered being unfaithful.

During the past year Jim has been under a lot of stress at the office and he's afraid he may lose his job. The tension caused by his career worries has taken its toll on their relationship. He never takes Sarah out anymore, and is so tired when he comes home that he hardly talks to her or the children.

Perhaps the greatest change has been in their sex life. Jim works late into the night at his computer until Sarah has gone to sleep. He doesn't give her compliments like he used to, and she no longer feels attractive to him. The extra ten pounds she's gained makes her feel even more unattractive and that Jim's lack of attention is all her fault. And when Jim does want to have sex, there's no intimacy or romance involved. He is just going through the motions, and as a result, she feels used.

Sarah has tried to talk to Jim on a number of occasions, but he makes her feel she is putting even more pressure on him. So Sarah just goes on quietly as though nothing is wrong. She prays things will change; she doesn't know what else to do.

Just when things are at their worst and Sarah is having serious concerns about her marriage, something happens at her part-time job. The doctor she works for seems to notice her for the first time. He compliments her new haircut. He tells her often how valuable she is to him, how much she has contributed to the smooth operation of his practice. Even more surprising, she catches him looking her way at odd times during the day.

All of a sudden, Sarah is much more aware of her boss. She notices his great physique. *I wonder if he works out at the gym,* she asks herself. She begins to realize what a brilliant doctor he is. *How can someone so smart appreciate the small contribution I make twice a week? I do a lot more for Jim, but he never seems to appreciate any of it!* She knows it's not right, but she just can't help but compare the two men. Why doesn't her husband treat her with the same respect her boss does?

One day it dawns on her that her boss is hitting on her. She feels a little guilty, but boy does his attention feel good! She blushes with pleasure whenever she catches him looking at her. Sarah starts taking more care with the way she dresses and with her makeup. She stops short of flirting, but is finding more excuses to interact with her boss.

As the weeks go by, Sarah finds herself thinking about the doctor more and more — even on the days she's home. She has a vivid dream about him, and it's not the kind she could share with anyone. She imagines what it would be like to be loved by such a handsome, rich, and powerful man.

Then the day comes when everything changes — though nothing really changes. The doctor asks Sarah out to lunch. It's just the most natural thing in the world, right? He wants to show his appreciation for her hard work.

Sarah contemplates accepting this "innocent" invitation. Her palms are sweaty and her heart is pounding, but she feels more alive than she has in months. *Can this be wrong? It would just be an innocent little one-hour lunch.*

Sarah never went any further with her boss, but she has already succumbed to several temptations. First, she gave in to the temptation of unhealthy comparison. She compared her husband to her handsome boss, and this magnified Jim's shortcomings and caused her to feel dissatisfied with him. She also gave in to the temptation of complacency — she gave up on her troubled marriage and didn't try to fix things. Instead, she focused on her own unhappiness. Add to that a generous dose of selfishness and negativity, and just a pinch of sexual fantasy, and she had a recipe for sin.

Why did she let herself get so emotionally involved with another man? Because her boss made her feel wanted and desirable while Jim made her feel rejected. The fantasy of following through with a physical encounter with the doctor was far more exciting than the disappointing sex she was having with Jim. The allure of the inappropriate relationship held Sarah tightly in its grip long before the "good" doctor asked her out. Temptation is always subtle.

It Always Tests Us

Just like exams we took in school, temptation comes in all shapes and sizes — but every temptation is a test. When we are given the opportunity and strong desire to act in a way we know we shouldn't, our faith, our obedience, our character, our self-discipline, our devotion to God, and other aspects of our nature are being put to the test. What will we do?

All of us are confronted daily with the little "pop quizzes"—the temptation to lose our tempers, be selfish or unkind, or neglect our time with the Lord. Other temptations test us in more challenging ways because resisting them requires that we make an uncomfortable choice. I faced such a temptation just recently.

I had been shopping with a friend at a home decorator store, and had gathered a basket of goodies for a bedroom and bath I was redoing. While my friend and I were shopping, we heard a loud noise and realized we were in the midst of a violent rainstorm. We looked out the front doors and saw that the wind was blowing and the sky was dark. We waited a few minutes, but the rain continued, so we decided to leave and make a run for it.

The short run to the car left us soaked. Just as we were shoving bags of candles and silk plants into the back seat, I noticed two large items on the bottom of the cart. With a sinking feeling I realized I had not paid for them. Would I do the right thing? Or would I do the comfortable thing? On this occasion I passed the test. I gathered the soggy items in my arms and made another run back into the store. Still, I wonder if my friend hadn't been with me, would I have thrown those items into the car and saved myself getting even wetter? The temptation to steal or be dishonest is a serious test.

Some of the temptations that come into our lives can only be called big, horrible, scary exams. Sarah's final temptation would fit into this category. Though she had already yielded to other temptations, the big test came when the doctor invited her to lunch.

Your big test might look completely different from Sarah's. You may have to choose whether to take part in vicious gossip that can destroy someone's reputation or ministry. Or perhaps you have to decide whether to return to an activity or lifestyle that God has clearly revealed is wrong. Your big test may be the temptation to give up on God and walk away from your faith when tragedy comes and your prayers are not being answered. Or your faith may be tested to the limit as you struggle to have a positive attitude, submit your life to God's plan, and refuse to be overcome by despair when you receive bad news or a serious medical diagnosis.

Such tests require great strength of character, brutal honesty, steely determination, and the ability to do hand-to-hand combat with Satan himself. They require every weapon of defense we can muster, because if we yield to these temptations, the results can be disastrous. Loved ones can suffer, churches can be divided, lives and ministries destroyed. And worst of all, our fellowship with God can be broken.

It Can Escalate

The last characteristic of temptation is that it escalates. It usually begins with small, subtle enticements. But each time we give in, the perceived reward gets more and more irresistible. We must learn to recognize the hidden snares of the Enemy before our "little sins" turn into huge ones. James tells us, "Then desire when it has conceived gives birth to sin; and sin when it is full-grown brings forth death" (1:15, RSV).

I recently interviewed a former stripper and drug addict. She said, "I was a cocktail waitress who said she'd never strip. Then a stripper who said she'd never trick." Eventually this woman ended up as a prostitute openly soliciting johns in the back alleys of New Orleans. Fortunately, hers is a story of God's redeeming power to change a life, but it also shows how temptation escalates.

The Characteristics of Temptation

- It offers us something we want.
- It is oh so subtle.
- It always tests us.
- It can escalate.

The better we understand temptation and how it works, the more likely we will be able to recognize when we are being tempted.

RECOGNIZING TEMPTATION

The woman who is most likely to yield to temptation is the one who doesn't recognize when she is being tempted to sin. When a woman is faithful to her husband (or remains pure in her singleness), active in her church, and tries to be a good mother, she can become spiritually overconfident and think she is somehow exempt from temptation. Because of this, she lets her guard down, gives in to temptation, and drifts into sinful behaviors so subtle that she doesn't even realize what she is doing is wrong.

In his book *Secrets of the Secret Place*, Bob Sorge makes a case for the importance of immediate repentance when we sin. He says:

> I am not thinking of repenting from sins like lying, fornication, stealing, cursing, pornography, hatred, drunkenness, or not tithing . . . Sincerity and a clear conscience doesn't even begin until we deal with these kinds of outward sins. . . . I am talking about repenting from our *iniquities*. . . . Iniquities are wrapped up in much more *subtle* areas of sinfulness, such as pride, rebellion, unbelief, envy, selfishness, and covetousness.[2]

Bob has hit the problem squarely on the head. Because we don't have huge sins in our lives, we think we are okay. With most of us it's not adultery, cheating, lying, addictions, or other obvious sins that bring us down. It's the sins we fall into without even realizing it.

Instead of resisting temptation, we give in to it and develop sinful patterns and behaviors without recognizing them for what they really are. We think of them as bad habits, or slight character flaws, or something we just inherited from our parents. We say, "It's just my personality." Or we sweep things under the rug by saying, "Well, I'm only human" or "I'm a work in progress." Ultimately, we fail to recognize the line between temptation and sin.

The Line Between Temptation and Sin

I wish I could give you a formula for knowing the exact moment you step across the line of temptation into sin. As we consider specific temptations in the following chapters, I will try to help you recognize where that line is, but this is not a black-and-white issue. The line can differ with each woman.

When you climb under the covers with a man before you're married to him, or with a man other than your husband, that's clearly sin. But what about sexual fantasies? If you have an adulterous thought about a man, does that constitute sin? Not if it happens against your will, but what you do with that thought can certainly become sinful. Was my jealousy of Tammy and Michelle a sin when I didn't even realize what was happening? Not at first, but once God showed me the problem, I was responsible for resisting the thought process that could lead to envy or jealousy. Are you sinning when you allow your controlling nature to create contention and strife, even though it's your God-given personality? It depends on where you are spiritually, and if you are aware of what you're doing.

Also, what is sin to one person may not be a sin to another. I'm not talking about the Ten Commandments here. But in more subtle areas of temptation, what may be an innocent mistake to one woman may constitute an act of sinful disobedience to another. The first time we are confronted with a temptation, we may not realize what is happening, but if the pattern of yielding to that temptation continues, we are without excuse.

Notice what the writers of James and Hebrews have to say:

Remember, too, that knowing what is right to do, and then not doing it is sin. (James 4:17, TLB)

If we deliberately keep on sinning after we have received the knowledge of the truth, no sacrifice for sins is left. (Hebrews 10:26)

However, the Holy Spirit will always reveal to us our sin if we keep an open heart and a tender and sensitive conscience and keep open lines of communication through prayer, meditation, and worship.

THE GOOD NEWS

Wherever I go I find that women have a deep desire to live above sin and temptation, provide wholesome role models for their children, and live purposeful and fruitful lives for God. They want a closer walk with God. Women flock to Christian conferences by the thousands, and it is obviously more than a desire to hang out for a day with their girlfriends.

But it's not enough to *desire* to please God and draw close to Him. Our lives must *demonstrate* that desire. God does not expect us to be perfect. He loves us with an everlasting love; He is patient and forgiving. But we must never forget that sin separates us from God and spoils our fellowship with Him. We should seek to identify the sin in our lives that keeps us from the intimacy and fellowship God intended for us.

The good news is that none of us have to succumb to The Eve Factor. God desires that we live in freedom and joy, and He has given us the spiritual resources to win over temptation and sin. "Greater is he that is in you, than he that is in the world" (1 John 4:4, KJV). We *can* live guilt-free lives of joy and purpose. "We are more than conquerors through him who loved us" (Romans 8:37).

Wherever you are in your spiritual journey, God loves you just where you are. No matter how many times you yield to temptation, if you go to God with a truly repentant heart, He will always forgive. "If we confess our sins, he is faithful and just and will forgive us our sins and purify us from all unrighteousness" (1 John 1:9).

This book is for the thousands of women who are entangled in the snare of the Enemy and may not even realize it. In the following chapters we will examine some specific areas of temptation so that you can:

- recognize when you are being tempted
- identify which temptations you are most vulnerable to and why
- build safeguards that can help you resist temptation
- develop godly qualities that make you less susceptible to temptation

In the following pages you'll find practical ways to recognize the danger signs and resist the temptations all women face. And you will find help for breaking through to a life of joy and success and a walk of holiness that gives pleasure to the Lord.

Why do you struggle with some temptations and not others? Why do you keep making the same mistakes over and over? Why do you succumb to certain sins that are not a problem for someone else—and vice versa? Keep reading to find out why you do the things you do.

CHAPTER ONE:
IT'S NOT ALWAYS ABOUT SEX

Study and Explore

Read the following Scriptures to expand your study of the Enemy of our souls. Write down what each verse tells you about him.

Example: Genesis 3:1—He was the shrewdest (or craftiest) of all God's creations.

Isaiah 14:12-14
Luke 10:18
2 Corinthians 11:14
2 Corinthians 12:7
1 Peter 5:8
Revelation 12:9

Consider and Reflect

1. How did Lucifer fall? What was his sin? (Isaiah 14:12-14)

2. What does Satan look like? (Ephesians 6:11-12; 2 Corinthians 11:14)

3. Should Christians be afraid of Satan? (1 John 4:4; Romans 8:37)

4. What temptations did Eve succumb to? (Genesis 3:6)

5. What is another word for temptation?

6. Is it a sin to be tempted? How do you know? (Mark 1:13)

7. Explain the difference between temptation and sin.

8. Do you believe Satan is as real as God?

9. Have you ever had the sense Satan was speaking to you or trying to get you to do something? Describe what happened, including your response.

10. If you feel afraid or intimidated by Satan, consider these promises: "Fear not, for I am with you. Do not be dismayed. I am your God. I will strengthen you; I will help you; I will uphold you with my victorious right hand" (Isaiah 41:10, TLB), and "Greater is he that is in you, than he that is in the world" (1 John 4:4, KJV).

11. The following is a list of problem areas that may be the result of temptation and sin. Circle the ones you struggle with.

   - Guilt or disconnection with God
   - Lack of peace
   - Strife-filled household
   - Marriage problems
   - Difficulty with children
   - Worry or fear
   - Pride
   - Undisciplined lifestyle
   - Misplaced priorities
   - No purpose in life
   - Discontentment

- Envy or jealousy
- Spiritual lethargy or coldness
- Lack of concern for others' spiritual needs
- Other _____

If we are honest, we can all identify areas of temptation in our lives. As you read this book, look for the ones that you struggle with and ask God to give you the strength to overcome them. If you sincerely want to live above sin, God will give you the power to resist.

Pray

Lord Jesus, I admit I fail You daily and will never measure up completely to Your standard of holiness. But I know You died on the cross so I wouldn't have to. I thank You that every sin is under Your blood. But I also ask that You show me the parts of my life that are not pleasing to You — those things I do that place a barrier between us. Help me to be especially aware of the work of Satan in my life. Give me power to defeat the Devil through Your name. Help me learn to resist the Enemy and be victorious over the little sins as well as the big sins in my life. In Your name, Amen.

WHY IS THIS SUCH A PROBLEM FOR ME?

How Your Temperament Makes You Vulnerable

*I don't understand myself at all, for I really want to do what is right,
but I can't. I do what I don't want to--what I hate.*

ROMANS 7:15 (TLB)

All of us are a composite of our background, memories, will, spiritual condition, and other factors. We also have unique needs, strengths, and weaknesses that make us more likely to succumb to certain temptations. We are multifaceted individuals whose reactions to a given situation, including possible temptations, are influenced by who we are.

For example, I have a friend who had quite a rocky time in her youth. As a teenager she became addicted to drugs and alcohol. Though God miraculously turned her life around, alcohol is still a strong temptation for my friend. She used alcohol as a crutch for so long that in times of stress or loneliness, she is still tempted to drink too much.

I, on the other hand, have never been tempted in this way because I grew up in a home with a lot of drinking. I have too many painful memories of the trauma and heartbreak that accompanies the abuse of alcohol. However, as you saw in the last chapter, I am susceptible to the temptation of unhealthy comparison. My vulnerability to this particular temptation stems, in part, from the feelings of inferiority I developed as a child. My background makes me vulnerable to temptations that are not a problem for others.

The better we understand ourselves, the more effective we can be at arming ourselves against those temptations that are more likely to bring us down. Many years ago I read a book that was not only fun and fascinating, it changed my life. It opened my eyes to what makes me tick and why I act the way I do. It helped me discover my greatest needs, my greatest challenges, and my strengths and weaknesses. I marveled as I recognized myself on those pages over and over again. The book? Florence Littauer's *Personality Plus*. After I finished reading it, I read all the books I could find on personality and temperament.

I've come to believe that our God-given temperaments are the greatest contributor to why we act and react the way we do and why we are more vulnerable to certain temptations. In fact, it's my opinion that we cannot be completely successful in our battle with temptation until we discover this one critically important truth about ourselves. For this reason, I strongly recommend that you delve into this helpful and fascinating study, beginning with *Personality Plus*.

Of course, knowing yourself better won't mean you will face fewer temptations. Believe me, Satan knows how you're wired, and he will use that knowledge against you every time. However, as you get to know yourself you can be on guard and work on your areas of weakness. You can discover what needs you have that sometimes override your desire to do what's right. Knowledge is *power*, and in this case it's power to overcome the temptations of the Enemy.

Nor will you be able to change your personality. I believe our personality type was God-designed, just like our size, shape, coloring, and other physical characteristics. Though we certainly change and grow during our lifetime, our basic nature remains the same. Florence calls it our "raw material."

> We start with our own set of inborn traits. Some of our qualities are beautiful with strains of gold. Some are blemished with fault lines of gray. Our circumstances, IQ, nationality, economics, environment, and parental influence can mold our personalities, but the rock underneath remains the same.[1]

With that said, let's move to a brief overview of the four personality types—the Popular Sanguine, the Perfect Melancholy, the Powerful Choleric, and the Peaceful Phlegmatic. We'll take a look at each of their strengths, weaknesses, and the areas of temptation each temperament is most vulnerable to. (Be sure to use the Personality Profile on pages 48-51 to determine which category or *combination of categories* you fit into.)

The Popular Sanguine

Strengths

Have you ever wondered why some people are almost always in a good mood? It's likely because of their temperament. Popular Sanguines are usually happy and upbeat.

I'm a Popular Sanguine and I've been told I am "disgustingly cheerful." At times my cheerfulness is annoying to other people, especially those who, because of their temperament, tend not to be cheerful. Often when I am really into a story, talking and laughing too loudly and too long, my niece Tara, who is a Melancholy/Choleric, will say, "Would someone please give her a Sanguine pill?" She says it good-naturedly, but I get the point.

31

Sanguines don't have the best memories, especially when it comes to names, dates, and places, but they do have an amazing penchant for details. They notice clothing, colors, jewelry, professions, decorating effects, hair styles, and shoes—details others might miss.

They are naturally inquisitive, as illustrated by this story Florence tells about a Sanguine who was having her roof reshingled and wanted to see how it was done. To the horror of the workers, she climbed up the ladder to the roof. The workers tried to convince her to get down before she hurt herself, but she was determined to see how they did their job. One of the men helped her over to the chimney, where she could sit and observe without being in the way. But she asked so many questions and gestured with so much enthusiasm that she lost her balance and fell backward into the chimney. It took four men to pull her out. She scraped her back on the bricks and her white pants were covered with soot. As the foreman helped her over to the ladder he said, "Look, Ma'am, we don't need your Mary Poppins act up here."[2]

Sanguines are rarely prone to be negative or critical. They are warm, friendly, and love physical contact. They love to tell stories and draw people in. Sanguines are the life of the party and, above all else, they know how to have fun. They can turn almost any dull and boring activity into an adventure.

Popular Sanguines have a great need to please others, be accepted and appreciated. This makes them pleasant and outgoing and able to get along well with others.

Weaknesses

Sanguines usually talk too much. They are not good listeners and are poor with follow-through. Most of them have an overinflated view of themselves, and can be vain and self-centered. Because of their need to be accepted, they tend to be followers instead of leaders.

Greatest Temptations

While a Sanguine's fun-loving nature is a plus, their desire for a good time can also get them into trouble. The search for "fun at any cost" can encourage them to go where they shouldn't go, do what they know is wrong, and be with people who are not a positive influence. Their need for acceptance makes them more likely to go along with the crowd as it's difficult for them to take a stand. The allure of being accepted along with having a good time makes them vulnerable to compromise and conformity.

Their desire to be liked, combined with their love of story-telling, makes them vulnerable to exaggeration. This was true for the wife of a colleague of mine. She used to get so carried away with telling stories that she would often exaggerate the facts. She so loved being the center of attention that she would exaggerate the story to make it even better—after all, she didn't want anyone to be bored! But the moment her stories meandered from the absolute truth, she crossed the line into sin. When the Holy Spirit convicted her of this, she asked her husband to pray with her and for her so that she would not give in to this temptation. Her accountability to a caring husband helped her to curb and resist this temptation.

Our attention to detail makes us Sanguines more susceptible to the temptation of inappropriate comparison. If you are not tuned in to what others have, wear, look like, or achieve, you are less likely to let it bother you. But, believe me, Sanguines *do* notice, and are more prone to sin in the areas of dissatisfaction, jealousy, and envy than any of the other temperaments. Their great need to be noticed, to be accepted, and to please others makes them put too much emphasis on appearance, clothes, and jewelry, making them more likely to fall victim to materialism.

Sanguines are eager to improve their behavior because they love new challenges and sincerely want to please and not offend. But difficulty with follow-through makes it unlikely that they will change, making them susceptible to the temptation of complacency and spiritual lethargy. Oh, they may be well aware of their spiritual need and sincerely resolve to have a better prayer life, spend more time in Bible study, or start a ministry. They may even begin with great excitement. But if the enthusiasm wanes and peters out after two weeks, they have ultimately yielded to the temptation of complacency.

Don't think for a moment, Sanguine sisters, that Satan won't bring every distraction possible to keep you from following through on your commitment to change sinful behaviors. He can keep you spiritually weak and ineffective by simply presenting you with too many choices. Overcommitment, busyness, and a frantic lifestyle are ploys the Enemy uses against all women. But it works especially well on us Sanguines.

Our overinflated view of ourselves can also keep us from changing—we can't see any of our flaws! A Sanguine's pride, ego, and self-centeredness can cause a lot of strife and can alienate others—even those we are trying so hard to please.

But Popular Sanguines, take heart! There is hope for us. Below (and at the end of each personality section) is a short list of a typical Sanguine's weaknesses and possible solutions to those weaknesses. I have also added a column of temptations most common to that personality type. Resisting and overcoming temptation usually involves a more complex spiritual solution, discipline, and much prayer. The last chapter of this book deals with overcoming temptation. But the solutions listed below are important because they may help neutralize our personality quirks that make us more vulnerable to temptation. These simple charts are by no means complete but are provided as a summary and to give you a highlight of what is to come in the following chapters.

Quick Reference Chart for Sanguines

WEAKNESS	SOLUTION	TEMPTATIONS
Self-centered	Be sensitive to others	Pride, Ego, Strife
Poor listener	Learn to Listen	Selfishness, Materialism Misplaced priorities
Talk too much	Talk half as much Stop exaggerating	Exaggerate to the point of lying
Uncultivated memories	Pay attention to names Write things down Make note of where you leave things (like the car and the children)	Complacency and the inability to grow or improve
Lack of follow-through	Be accountable to others	

THE PERFECT MELANCHOLY

Strengths

Perfect Melancholies, who are the opposite of Popluar Sanguines, are usually serious and always have a plan. They may procrastinate beginning the plan for years, but they *always* have a plan.

My oldest son Jeff is a Melancholy. When he was about six years old his dad asked him what he wanted to be when he grew up. When Jeff hesitated, Jerry said, "Wouldn't you like to go into Christian television (like your dad)?"

"No, Dad," Jeff replied. I want to do something *important*, like be a scientist or an archaeologist." Today, Jeff is an archaeologist, specializing in ancient languages.

Perfect Melancholies have an abundance of strengths. They are often more gifted, creative, and brilliant than the other types. They give us our art, culture, literature, philosophy, and great music. Their need for perfection prevents them from ever settling for mediocrity. They crave order and organization and take extremely good care of their things—at least the things that are important to them.

I can vividly remember one stressful night before Jerry, Jeff, and I left for a trip to Israel. Jeff was traveling over with us, but would remain in Israel the next year, studying Hebrew. After an exhausting day of packing, tying up loose ends, and helping get Jeff ready to move away for a year, I was hoping to get a few good hours of sleep. However, it did not happen. Jeff spent the night carrying boxes of his books, his most treasured possession, up a ladder to the attic. Clomp, clomp, bang, bang—all night long. I could not convince him to leave them on the shelves in his room, where they had been arranged perfectly, cataloged, and recorded. He told me later he wasn't taking any chances that while he was away I might decide to redecorate his room and put his books into the basement where they might get flooded. A typical Melancholy, he had anticipated the worst-case scenario.

Unlike Sanguines, who will do almost anything to make friends and not offend anyone, Melancholies usually appear a little "different," and take pleasure in their eccentricities. They don't mind bucking the system and are rarely tempted to compromise their standards to fit in.

Melancholies are not social animals by nature and usually don't have a lot of friends. But they are wonderful, loyal, friends to the few they do have. They are caring and sensitive, even sacrificial, and focus much on others.

Weaknesses

Though unselfish, talented, and organized, Melancholies have their own share of weaknesses and problems. Though they have the most creative potential, they are sometimes their own worst enemy. Unlike the Phlegmatic, who procrastinates because she thinks she might get out of doing something, Melancholies procrastinate because they want to do things perfectly.[3]

They are often gloomy and easily depressed, and because they enjoy their depression, they don't want to be cheered up. This is true of Jeff, and I used to worry that he was so sad. In a household of happy, optimistic people, Jeff was like a dark cloud. I stopped worrying about him when I learned this was normal behavior for a Melancholy.

Melancholies can think everyone else is slightly inferior to them, but it doesn't result in an ego problem. They also judge themselves more harshly than they do others, which often causes them to have low self-esteem. More than anything else, Perfect Melancholies have a tremendous need for perfection. They demand far too much from others and from themselves.

Greatest Temptations

As Christians we have every reason to be positive, hopeful, and full of faith and joy. But this mindset doesn't come easy for Melancholies, who have a great susceptibility to the temptation to be negative.

My friend Grace, who is a Melancholy, can attest to this. For years she served as the assistant to the principal of a private school. Her attention to detail and her perfectionism made her very good at what she did. However, a year ago, things began to change. Some disgruntled parents started making accusations against the principal. The stories got ugly, and the owner of the school hired a new principal, but Grace's boss was given the option to stay until the end of the year. She chose to stay.

When the parents and teachers rallied behind the new inexperienced principal, Grace's boss became very angry, demanding, vindictive, and even paranoid. At the same time the office staff was reduced, which greatly increased Grace's workload.

Everyone took sides and Grace found herself caught in the middle. The school became a den of vicious gossip, jealousy, threats, anger, calls to the ACLU and the police, and hurt feelings. It would have been difficult for anyone to work in that environment, but Grace's Melancholy penchant for order and perfection made the situation unbearable. She would call me each week almost in despair, sharing every tiny detail of her ordeal. Her stressful work situation crowded out all the good things in her life, and she made everyone around her miserable, too. Thankfully, Grace was able to retire at the end of the year and was spared any further involvement. She readily admits she yielded to the temptation of negativity, making a bad situation even worse.

As Grace discovered, trust in God can be challenging for a Melancholy. If this is your temperament, please remember that life does get messy. You can only control your circumstances to a point — then you have to hand them to God and move on.

Melancholy reader, Satan can use your penchant for pessimism to rob you of joy and peace. He will use your perfectionism to prevent you from accomplishing what God has called you to do and your obsession with minute details to cause you to miss the big picture and get your priorities out of order. He will cause worry to rob you of faith. But you *can* change.

Recognize your weakness and then ask God to give you a new perspective. Ask Him to help you see the big picture and not obsess about the tiny details. *Don't sweat the small stuff.* God can help you establish new patterns of happiness and confidence.

Quick Reference Chart for Melancholies

WEAKNESS	SOLUTION	TEMPTATIONS
Easily Depressed	Look for the positives Don't get feelings hurt	Negativity, Fear, Lack of faith
Low self-esteem	Memorize God's promises Focus on your strengths Interact with encouraging, upbeat people	Fall short of spiritual potential
Procrastinate	Gather the right things before you start Spend less time planning	Put off or disobey what God tells you to do
Put unrealistic demands on others and yourself	Accept others as they are Accept your own limitations Relax your standards	Create strife Criticism, Gossip Fail to love others
Obsess about the small things	Ask God for a new perspective	Miss the big picture and God's plan

THE POWERFUL CHOLERIC

Strengths

Have you ever sat through a fund-raising banquet or other event and found yourself thinking how much better *you* could have planned the event? It happens to me all the time. In addition to being a Popular Sanguine, I'm also a Powerful Choleric. Most people are a combination of at least two types, although it's possible to have some characteristics from all four types.

Cholerics are born leaders and most heads of state, corporate presidents, politicians, and movers and shakers of any organization fit into this category. They love solving problems and being the one with the answer. When presented with a dilemma, a Choleric will come up with a solution in short order—even if it's wrong. But usually they *are* right. They are confident and decisive and must be constantly *doing*.

Florence Littauer puts it this way:

> While Popular Sanguine is talking and Perfect Melancholy is thinking, Powerful Choleric is achieving. He is the easiest temperament to understand and get along with, as long as you live by his golden rule: Do it my way NOW!"[4]

Powerful Cholerics have a tremendous need for accomplishment. They are excellent organizers and extremely good in emergencies. They are goal-oriented and can run anything. They don't mind confrontation and love to speak up for what is right. A Choleric is practical, not easily discouraged, and can motivate others.

Weaknesses

Many Cholerics aren't well liked because of their aggressiveness and because they are usually right. But if a woman is a combination of both Choleric and Sanguine temperaments, she can be more fun-loving and accommodating and still get the job done.[5] I thank God for the Sanguine part of my personality, because without it, I would be such a bossy know-it-all, no one could stand to be around me.

Like sandpaper, Cholerics can grate on those around them. They are the leaders, the type As, the control freaks of this world. They are hard-working and can accomplish great things. But they often leave bleeding victims in their wake.

Cholerics are workaholics because they *enjoy* working. Even when they are at rest, which is far too infrequent, they are thinking about all that needs to be done. But this plays havoc with relationships as they would rather be working than socializing.

A Choleric does everything fast — talk, walk, and process information. This tends to make them impatient and sometimes abrupt with others who do not move or think as fast as they do. If you are Choleric, keep in mind that whether it's your spouse, your employees, your children or friends, others do not appreciate your wisdom and cleverness when it's forced on them. They do not relish being made to feel stupid, inferior, or guilty for not accomplishing as much as you. They don't want you to be right all the time. In fact, you might be surprised at how others secretly want you to fail, just to prove you can fall off your high horse down to their level!

Greatest Temptations

The task-driven Choleric is always tempted to put work, career, or just *activity* above people. My niece Tara, a classic Choleric, realized that she had succumbed to this temptation after a foot injury forced her to walk very slowly. An attorney and a high-powered leader who managed projects and people, her normal practice was to go blazing through the building at warp speed, barely speaking to those she passed.

Having to slow down annoyed her at first because people started stopping in the hallway to chat with her. They felt more comfortable approaching her and making small talk. To her surprise she found herself enjoying getting to know her colleagues and building relationships with them. They shared what was happening in their lives and she began to open up about hers.

Before her injury, Tara had seen people only as a means to an end, a necessary element in completing her objectives. She unknowingly used people. She believed the lie that it was okay to bulldoze others to get the job done. However, she didn't accomplish more; she accomplished less. But when she started taking time to build relationships, the employees on her team became more cooperative.

Her projects came together easier. She no longer had to hunt every-one down and make things happen, because people sought her out and her productivity improved.

The Choleric's fast pace can get him out of sync with God's timetable. He can easily let life get out of balance, because activities such as relaxing, prayer, studying the Bible, or cultivating friendships don't come easy.

More than any other type, Cholerics are the most likely to create strife and contention. Their know-it-all attitude alienates people, and their controlling natures can cause friction in a marriage or at the office. They are leaders, not followers, and because they can persuade others to their way of thinking, they can be divisive. Many churches have been split because disgruntled Cholerics could not keep their dissatisfaction to themselves.

When Cholerics have strong opinions about something—and they always have strong opinions—they have a compulsion to sway others to their way of thinking. Their self-confidence, competence, and independence—which are strengths—are also areas of greatest vulnerability and make them susceptible to the sin of pride. This sin not only ruins relationships with others, it can become a barrier to relationship with God. Pride says *I can do it on my own. I don't need God or anyone else.* "Pride goes before destruction, a haughty spirit before a fall" (Proverbs 16:18).

Finally, Cholerics must guard against the temptation of misplaced priorities and compromise. Their ambition and strong desire for accomplishment can crowd out spiritual and family commitments. A workaholic personality tempts them to do too much and often gets their lives out of balance. And, if they aren't careful, they can compromise character and standards because they are driven to succeed at any cost.

Choleric sisters, in spite of many shortcomings, God can use your gifts for Christ's kingdom. However, you must first realize you *do* have faults and are *not* always right. You must pull back your strong personality, seek true humility, and learn to submit to God's plan and purpose.

Quick Reference Chart for Cholerics

WEAKNESS	SOLUTION	TEMPTATIONS
Workaholics	Learn to relax Take pressure off others Plan leisure time	Overactivity Misplaced priorities
Must be in control	Submit to others and God Don't look down on anyone Stop manipulating	Dominate others Arrogance, Selfishness
Not good with people	Practice patience Don't give unsolicited advice Pull back, don't come on so strong Don't be confrontational	Create strife and contention Make others angry
Always right	Let others be right sometimes Learn to apologize Admit your faults	Pride, ego, unteachable spirit
Impatient	Realize others move slower Seek to move in God's timing	Get ahead of God

THE PEACEFUL PHLEGMATIC

Strengths

Peaceful Phlegmatics are calm, cool, and collected in almost any situation. This personality type is the best suited for parenting because Phlegmatics are usually soft-spoken, soothing, and patient. My Phlegmatic daughter, Vanessa, is the mother of five children, two with special needs, and she is actively planning to adopt more. Peaceful Phlegmatics can manage a house full of children with efficiency, finesse, and poise.

They are careful never to invade your space. Unlike the Popular Sanguine, who will do anything to be noticed, and the Powerful Choleric, who can't help but be noticed, the Peaceful Phlegmatic has no need for attention and avoids it. I can't tell you how many times I have walked into a room, looked around, and said, "Where's Vanessa?" I will hear her sigh disgustedly and finally see her waving at me. She was sitting right under my nose all the time, but I didn't notice her.

The Phlegmatic's greatest need is for peace, and they avoid conflict at all costs. They are the great stabilizers of this world. While the other temperaments have extreme highs and lows, the Phlegmatic keeps an even keel. They can put things in perspective with one soft-spoken sentence. They are a pleasure to be around because they don't put much pressure on themselves or others. They are not easily upset and realize most of the stressful situations we face are just not worth the trouble. They are flexible and roll with the punches. They have an uncanny way of cutting through the rhetoric and getting to the real issue.

Phlegmatic women are not flashy; their principle adornment is a meek and quiet spirit (see 1 Peter 3:4). They are rarely in a hurry, quiet and witty, and are good listeners.

Weaknesses

While every family should be blessed with at least one Phlegmatic, these easygoing, likable types come with their own set of draw-backs. Since they are natural followers, they can be easily swayed by the wrong people, especially in their youth.

Plegmatics are hard to motivate, often appear lazy, and will do as little as they can. They have a problem saying "no" to anyone. But unlike a Choleric who overcommits herself to projects and then kills herself to accomplish them, the Phlegmatic will *say* "yes," but not follow through with anything that involves too much work. They are terrible procrasti-nators. Why do today what you can put off until tomorrow?

Phlegmatics are not as negative as Melancholies, but since they are not impressed with much in life, they tend to be cynical and even sarcastic.

Once my family was driving to a restaurant when we noticed a homeless man digging through the garbage. Jeff, my sensitive Melancholy son, asked if we could stop and give the man some money. We did, and we were all feeling rather noble about it. Vanessa had been taking this all in without saying a word. Finally, she said, "Well, if he was so poor, how could he afford those glasses he was wearing?"

Though they seem easygoing, Phlegmatics are often stubborn and have a will of iron. They may appear to be cooperating, but they save their retaliation until a more opportune time and can punish by passive-aggressive behavior. They are prone to sulking and grudge-holding.

Greatest Temptations

Phlegmatics are tempted to get their lives out of balance — not by overactivity, but by underactivity. Because they are hard to motivate and don't like to take risks, they can miss God's best.

Perhaps more than any other personality type, Phlegmatics are integrated completely into the natural, everyday world and tend to be skeptical of the supernatural one. They don't get excited about many things, including the wonders God wants to perform in their lives. If given a chance, a Phlegmatic could rationalize away the parting of the Red Sea. Or they might yawn and say, "Well, it didn't help the Israelites much. God ended up killing most of them off in the desert anyway." Where others see miracles, they only see coincidences.

A Phlegmatic's greatest temptation is probably complacency. They are reluctant to try something new and can find a million excuses — even when the request comes from above. They are usually shy and fearful and prefer to stay in their comfort zone, no matter what. Their temptation can take the form of what they *fail* to do instead of what they *do*.

That was the case with Charlene, a lovely Phlegmatic acquaintance of mine. She told me she had a strong desire to attend a woman's Bible study, as she wanted to grow in her Christian walk and learn to witness to others. But she said she just couldn't make herself attend a study. She is not comfortable with praying in front of others, is insecure about her Bible knowledge, and too shy to venture out. She is frustrated with herself, but her fear of being put on the spot holds her back. I suggested she find a friend or two who she feels comfortable with to attend with her. She agreed, but I have a feeling she will still procrastinate.

This is a good example of a behavior that is not necessarily sin, but can still interfere with what God wants to do in a woman's life. Her complacency can hold Charlene back spiritually, and thus be an effective tool in the hands of the Enemy. If this tendency continues and touches other areas of her Christian walk, it could definitely come between Charlene and her relationship with Christ.

Charlene also told me that she had heard someone making serious accusations against a friend of hers. The gossip was vicious and Charlene knew much of what she was hearing was not true. However, her shyness and distaste for confrontation prevented her from speaking up. Later, she realized her silence was tantamount to agreeing with the gossip. Charlene was so convicted that she eventually went to the person and defended her friend. Her courage in doing so was commendable in light of the fact it put her way out of her comfort zone — *and* when you remember a Phlegmatic's greatest need is for peace.

If you are a Phlegmatic, you can probably find areas of complacency in your life. In order to guard against this temptation, you may need to develop some personal discipline, have some accountability partners, and pray for the courage to put yourself "out there." God will walk alongside you and give you the power to be obedient. Even Phlegmatics can get excited and get moving!

Quick Reference Chart for Phlegmatics

WEAKNESS	SOLUTION	TEMPTATIONS
Not Exciting	Try to get enthused	Settle for mediocrity
Resist Change	Try something new	Be disobedient to God's directives
Seem lazy	Accept responsibility Don't procrastinate Motivate yourself	Complacency Stay in your comfort zone
Quiet but stubborn	Communicate your feelings Be more open and teachable	Build a barrier against others, even God
Appear wishy-washy	Learn to make decisions Learn to say "no"	Procrastinate

KNOWLEDGE = POWER

If you want to build your resistance to temptation and overcome The Eve Factor, I cannot overemphasize the importance of learning about your God-given temperament. Use the Quick Reference Charts in this chapter and the Personality Profile on pages 48-51 to learn more about yourself and your greatest temptations.

As fascinating and insightful as a study of the personalities can be, however, we still need God's help to really understand ourselves thoroughly. We need to pray as the psalmist did:

> Search me, O God, and know my heart; test me, and know my anxious thoughts. See if there is any offensive way in me, and lead me in the way everlasting. (Psalm 139:23-24)

As you consider your personality, ask God to show you how Satan may be using your weaknesses and even your strengths against you. In the following chapters we will examine some specific temptations. As you read, ask the Lord to give you supernatural insight into all that makes you who you are.

Your Personality Profile

In each of the following rows of four words across, check the one or two words that most often applies to you. Continue through all forty lines. If you are not sure which word "most applies," ask a spouse or a friend, and think of what your answer would have been when you were a child — your natural personality.

Strengths

1 ○ Adventurous	○ Adaptable	○ Animated	○ Analytical
2 ○ Persistent	○ Playful	○ Persuasive	○ Peaceful
3 ○ Submissive	○ Self-sacrificing	○ Sociable	○ Strong-willed
4 ○ Considerate	○ Controlled	○ Competitive	○ Convincing
5 ○ Refreshing	○ Respectful	○ Reserved	○ Resourceful
6 ○ Satisfied	○ Sensitive	○ Self-reliant	○ Spirited
7 ○ Planner	○ Patient	○ Positive	○ Promoter
8 ○ Sure	○ Spontaneous	○ Scheduled	○ Shy
9 ○ Orderly	○ Obliging	○ Outspoken	○ Optimistic
10 ○ Friendly	○ Faithful	○ Funny	○ Forceful
11 ○ Daring	○ Delightful	○ Diplomatic	○ Detailed
12 ○ Cheerful	○ Consistent	○ Cultured	○ Confident
13 ○ Idealistic	○ Independent	○ Inoffensive	○ Inspiring
14 ○ Demonstrative	○ Decisive	○ Dry humor	○ Deep
15 ○ Mediator	○ Musical	○ Mover	○ Mixes easily
16 ○ Thoughtful	○ Tenacious	○ Talker	○ Tolerant
17 ○ Listener	○ Loyal	○ Leader	○ Lively
18 ○ Contented	○ Chief	○ Chartmaker	○ Cute
19 ○ Perfectionist	○ Pleasant	○ Productive	○ Popular
20 ○ Bouncy	○ Bold	○ Behaved	○ Balanced

Your Personality Profile

Weaknesses

21 ○ Blank	○ Bashful	○ Brassy	○ Bossy
22 ○ Undisciplined	○ Unsympathetic	○ Unenthusiastic	○ Unforgiving
23 ○ Reticent	○ Resentful	○ Resistant	○ Repetitious
24 ○ Fussy	○ Fearful	○ Forgetful	○ Frank
25 ○ Impatient	○ Insecure	○ Indecisive	○ Interrupts
26 ○ Unpopular	○ Uninvolved	○ Unpredictable	○ Unaffectionate
27 ○ Headstrong	○ Haphazard	○ Hard to please	○ Hesitant
28 ○ Plain	○ Pessimistic	○ Proud	○ Permissive
29 ○ Angered easily	○ Aimless	○ Argumentative	○ Alienated
30 ○ Naive	○ Negative attitude	○ Nervy	○ Nonchalant
31 ○ Worrier	○ Withdrawn	○ Workaholic	○ Wants credit
32 ○ Too sensitive	○ Tactless	○ Timid	○ Talkative
33 ○ Doubtful	○ Disorganized	○ Domineering	○ Depressed
34 ○ Inconsistent	○ Introvert	○ Intolerant	○ Indifferent
35 ○ Messy	○ Moody	○ Mumbles	○ Manipulative
36 ○ Slow	○ Stubborn	○ Show-off	○ Skeptical
37 ○ Loner	○ Lord over others	○ Lazy	○ Loud
38 ○ Sluggish	○ Suspicious	○ Short-tempered	○ Scatterbrained
39 ○ Revengeful	○ Restless	○ Reluctant	○ Rash
40 ○ Compromising	○ Critical	○ Crafty	○ Changeable

Now transfer all your selections to the corresponding words on the Personality Scoring Sheet and add up your totals.

For more information on the Personalities (as taught by Florence Littauer) or to order copies of the Personality Profile, please contact CLASServices at 800-433-6633 or visit www.classervices.com.

Personality Scoring Sheet

Name: _____

Now transfer all your X's to the corresponding words on the Personality Scoring Sheet, and add up your totals. For example, if you checked Animated on the profile, check it on the scoring sheet. (Note: The words are in a different order on the profile and the scoring sheet.)

Strengths

	Popular Sanguine	Powerful Choleric	Perfect Melancholy	Peaceful Phlegmatic
1	○ Animated	○ Adventurous	○ Analytical	○ Adaptable
2	○ Playful	○ Persuasive	○ Persistent	○ Peaceful
3	○ Sociable	○ Strong-willed	○ Self-sacrificing	○ Submissive
4	○ Convincing	○ Competitive	○ Considerate	○ Controlled
5	○ Refreshing	○ Resourceful	○ Respectful	○ Reserved
6	○ Spirited	○ Self-reliant	○ Sensitive	○ Satisfied
7	○ Promoter	○ Positive	○ Planner	○ Patient
8	○ Spontaneous	○ Sure	○ Scheduled	○ Shy
9	○ Optimistic	○ Outspoken	○ Orderly	○ Obliging
10	○ Funny	○ Forceful	○ Faithful	○ Friendly
11	○ Delightful	○ Daring	○ Detailed	○ Diplomatic
12	○ Cheerful	○ Confident	○ Cultured	○ Consistent
13	○ Inspiring	○ Independent	○ Idealistic	○ Inoffensive
14	○ Demonstrative	○ Decisive	○ Deep	○ Dry Humor
15	○ Mixes easily	○ Mover	○ Musical	○ Mediator
16	○ Talker	○ Tenacious	○ Thoughtful	○ Tolerant
17	○ Lively	○ Leader	○ Loyal	○ Listener
18	○ Cute	○ Chief	○ Chartmaker	○ Contented
19	○ Popular	○ Productive	○ Perfectionist	○ Pleasant
20	○ Bouncy	○ Bold	○ Behaved	○ Balanced

Totals: Strengths

Personality Scoring Sheet

Name: _____

Weaknesses

	Popular Sanguine	Powerful Choleric	Perfect Melancholy	Peaceful Phlegmatic
21	○ Brassy	○ Bossy	○ Bashful	○ Blank
22	○ Undisciplined	○ Unsympathetic	○ Unforgiving	○ Unenthusiastic
23	○ Repetitious	○ Resistant	○ Resentful	○ Reticent
24	○ Forgetful	○ Frank	○ Fussy	○ Fearful
25	○ Interrupts	○ Impatient	○ Insecure	○ Indecisive
26	○ Unpredictable	○ Unaffectionate	○ Unpopular	○ Uninvolved
27	○ Haphazard	○ Headstrong	○ Hard to please	○ Hesitant
28	○ Permissive	○ Proud	○ Pessimistic	○ Plain
29	○ Angered easily	○ Argumentative	○ Alienated	○ Aimless
30	○ Naive	○ Nervy	○ Negative attitude	○ Nonchalant
31	○ Wants credit	○ Workaholic	○ Withdrawn	○ Worrier
32	○ Talkative	○ Tactless	○ Too sensitive	○ Timid
33	○ Disorganized	○ Domineering	○ Depressed	○ Doubtful
34	○ Inconsistent	○ Intolerant	○ Introvert	○ Indifferent
35	○ Messy	○ Manipulative	○ Moody	○ Mumbles
36	○ Show-off	○ Stubborn	○ Skeptical	○ Slow
37	○ Loud	○ Lord over others	○ Loner	○ Lazy
38	○ Scatterbrained	○ Short-tempered	○ Suspicious	○ Sluggish
39	○ Restless	○ Rash	○ Revengeful	○ Reluctant
40	○ Changeable	○ Crafty	○ Critical	○ Compromising

Totals: Weaknesses

[ ]   [ ]   [ ]   [ ]

Combined Totals

[ ]   [ ]   [ ]   [ ]

CHAPTER TWO:
WHY IS THIS SUCH A PROBLEM FOR ME?

Study and Explore

The following Scriptures offer good advice for everyone, but they can be more applicable to certain temperaments. Write Sanguine, Choleric, Melancholy, or Phlegmatic next to the Scriptures that best apply.

Example: Galatians 5:13 — (Be willing to serve) Choleric
James 1:19 (Talk less)
Philippians 4:6 (Don't worry)
Philippians 4:8 (Be optimistic)
Galatians 5:22- 23 (Be joyful)
Proverbs 3:7 (Be humble)
1 Corinthians 16:13 (Be firm in your faith)
Ephesians 4:31 (Avoid gossip and bitterness)
Colossians 3:23 (Work harder)
Romans 12:10 (Put others first)
Galatians 5:22-23 (Be patient)

Consider and Reflect

1. What determines a person's temperament? Genetics or environment?

2. Is it possible to change your temperament? Why or why not?

3. How can we learn to pull back on our weaknesses and build on our strengths to become more Christlike?

4. How can a person's background and experience make him/her more vulnerable to temptation? Give an example from your own life.

5. Can Satan use our strengths as well as our weaknesses to bring temptation? How?

6. Take the personality test on pages 48-49 and do the following:

- Identify which personality type or combination best describes you.
- Identify which personality type or combination best describes your husband and children.
- Make a list of your weaknesses.
- Make a list of your strengths.
- List the temptations you have struggled with due to your temperament.
- What needs and tendencies do you have that sometimes overrule your desire to live a godly life? Take each of these to the Lord and ask for help in understanding why they are a snare in your life.

Pray

Dear Lord, help me to know myself. Show me anything in my past that I have not dealt with and bring healing and deliverance. Allow me to better understand the temperament You gave me and how I can maximize my strengths and minimize my weaknesses. Give me a teachable spirit and the power to change those areas of my life that displease You. Help me to accept others and be tolerant of their personalities. Help me to celebrate the way You made me and value myself because You love me. In Your name, Amen.

GREENER GRASS, GREED, AND THE GREEN-EYED MONSTER

The Temptation of Unhealthy Comparison

But they . . . comparing themselves among themselves, are not wise.
2 CORINTHIANS 10:12, KJV

love dishes and have cabinets full of them. I have collected dishes from flea markets, garage sales, and discount stores. While I have never owned an expensive set of fine china, I like all sorts of dinnerware, both new and antique. I recently changed the colors in my kitchen, which gave me an excuse for buying a new set of casual dishes. I found a set I loved; they were on sale, so I felt good about the purchase. The new, colorful dishes looked fantastic on my table. But just a few days later, I was in an upscale decorator store and saw a dish pattern I liked so much, it took away some of the pleasure of my new dishes.

Isn't this typical? We believe the lie that material possessions bring us joy, but our possessions are fleeting, and *things* never bring true happiness. Dissatisfaction is only a small part of the harvest of unhealthy comparison.

You may be thinking, *I know women struggle with a lot of temptations and sins, but is comparison a sin?* I realize I have just devoted an entire chapter to emphasizing the differences among us and how to recognize and appreciate those differences. So what's wrong with making comparisons when failing to do so would be blindness or total denial? Allow me to explain.

Just as it's possible to be angry and not sin, it's also possible to compare yourself with others and not sin. Comparing ourselves to others is a human response that can be used for both good and bad purposes. In fact, I just experienced a vivid comparison that had a positive outcome.

My husband and I have close friends in Romania. Tudor and Mirela were staunch Communists during Nicolae Ceausescu's reign of terror. After their dramatic conversion to Christ, they dedicated their telecommunications knowledge to establishing an effective Christian television ministry that reaches most of their country.

During our last visit to Romania, Tudor and Mirela invited us to come to their home of more than twenty-five years, a flat in one of the many institutional-looking apartment complexes Ceausescu built to house the population. He tore down private homes and moved everyone into these flats so that his informers could keep a close eye on the people. Their apartment has two small bedrooms, a living room, a tiny kitchen and bath. For over twenty years their two children slept in the bedrooms and they slept on a pull-out sofa in the small living area. We visited them shortly after their daughter had married, and Tudor and Mirela were happy to finally have a bedroom of their own.

As I sat in their humble home, I was ashamed of all the times I had succumbed to dissatisfaction over what I considered a small home, worn furniture, or ugly carpeting. I remembered all the times I have sat in someone's huge, gorgeous home and let tiny niggles of envy or dissatisfaction creep in. Sitting in this couple's modest living room, I couldn't help but compare my lovely home in the United States to their tiny apartment. The comparison made me grateful for my abundant blessings and helped me to truly appreciate these dedicated servants of God. When comparison results in gratitude and generosity, it is healthy and appropriate.

However, we rarely compare ourselves to people who are less privileged than we are. We are more likely to compare our possessions (or lives or children or looks or talents) with those who have more than we do. As a result, we experience *relative deprivation*. When we feel deprived based on what others have, our comparisons are unhealthy, they bear negative fruit, and we often fall into sin.

THE FRUIT OF INAPPROPRIATE COMPARISON

Many women don't realize they are being tempted in this area because unhealthy comparison can have different motivation and different consequences. Let's examine some of the negative fruits of this temptation.

Jealousy, Envy, and Greed

Envy and jealousy often result from inappropriate comparison and are perhaps the most unattractive of sins. At least lust, pride, anger, and the like have some satisfaction—though fleeting. Envy offers nothing but misery, unhappiness, and finally guilt.[1] How do you know if you have allowed envy, jealousy, or greed to creep in?

Recognizing the Temptation

Here are some ways we make unhealthy comparisons that can result in jealousy, envy, or greed. Have you ever had thoughts like these?

- My daughter is just as cute and school-spirited as the girl next door, so why didn't she get chosen for the cheerleading squad?

- I'm more attractive and a much better wife than my friend, so why is her husband more loving and attentive? My husband never brings me flowers.
- It is so unfair that our friends just bought a lake cabin when we struggle to pay our mortgage.

Many women don't see thoughts like these for what they are: jealousy and envy. They write such feelings off as something all woman experience—*it's just a woman thing.* On top of that, the media encourages us to think we deserve the things we don't have, and many of us have developed a sense of entitlement as a result. We couch our envy or greed in terms such as *healthy ambition* or *a desire to better ourselves.* But no matter how we try to justify or legitimize our envy, it's what Paul calls *a work of the flesh* (Galatians 5:19,21, KJV). Envy, or what Scripture often calls *covetousness*, is listed many times in the New Testament as a serious sin (see Mark 7:22; Luke 12:15; Romans 1:29; James 3:14). Colossians 3:5 calls it *idolatry.*

Envy and jealousy are powerful tools in the hands of the Enemy. Consider these examples from Scripture. Jealousy caused:

- Joseph's brothers to sell him into slavery and trick their father into thinking he was dead (Genesis 37).
- King Saul to try to kill David because the people of Israel loved him (1 Samuel 18:9-11).
- The Pharisees to persuade the Romans to crucify Jesus because of His popularity (Mark 3:6).

Don't ever excuse jealousy by saying, "It's just a woman thing." It is evil and destructive and high on the list of a woman's most common temptations. It's not only important to recognize jealousy and envy in our lives, but also to understand the temptation and what makes us vulnerable.

Understanding the Temptation

Women succumb to the sin of jealousy or envy for different reasons. Here are some sources of this temptation that help us to better understand why we are vulnerable.

1. Baggage from our background. When you consider my background, my personality, my insecurities, my memories, my failures, it's not hard to see why I succumbed to the temptation of unhealthy comparisons with Tammy and Michelle that resulted in jealousy.

I was born in the backwoods of Mississippi in humble circumstances. My parents were good, hard-working people, but they knew little about parenting. They didn't realize the importance of encouragement or affirmation. They worked much of the time, and my older sister cared for me. I was a skinny, cross-eyed little girl who wore glasses from the time I was four. My sister was more like my mother in temperament, and the one my mom relied on. I was flighty and absentminded. My mom and dad laughed at my little-girl antics, which I often used to get attention, but I don't think they took me seriously. I continuously tried to please my mother, but was never sure I did.

As I grew up, I made good grades, had many friends, and gained a certain amount of self-confidence. But even as a young teen, I still wore glasses, had bird legs, and was often teased by the boys in school. My low self-esteem improved over time, but even today it lies just below the surface and makes me vulnerable to the perceived payoff I'll gain if I compare myself to others to prove I measure up. (But as I pointed out earlier, it usually has the reverse effect.)

Every time I went on television with Tammy and Michelle, I compared myself to them and felt inadequate. I'd think, *We are all three writers, speakers, and television hosts, so why should Tammy and Michelle be selling more books than I? We all love the Lord and want to help women, so why are Michelle and Tammy speaking to thousands, while I only speak to hundreds (and often only dozens). We all have to look presentable on camera, but it is so much easier for them because they are younger and more attractive than I.*

Because of the baggage from my background, I yielded to unhealthy comparisons with them, and it was fertile ground for jealousy to grow. As they talked about their successes and opportunities, I wanted to be as good as they were. The allure of "being appreciated" and "being worthy" and "being their equal" was just too much to resist.

2. Our perception that others are disappointed in us. Another reason we succumb to the sin of jealousy is because we feel that *others* have compared us (our looks, popularity, talent, intelligence) to someone else and found us inferior. In reality, this may not be true, but that is our perception.

Betty and her brother John were close as children. But then Betty began to notice that John seemed to get more attention from their parents. Her perception was that her mom and dad loved her brother more. It wasn't true, but that is how she felt, and she was jealous of him.

Her jealousy grew when they entered high school and John became a star athlete and popular leader in their school. Betty was a beautiful girl but more introverted than her brother. She couldn't help but notice that everyone—her parents, their friends, the teachers—all seemed to favor him.

Later, as John's career took off, Betty felt even more insignificant, and her resentment toward her brother grew. After their parents' deaths Betty wanted nothing to do with John or his family. She felt vindicated by withholding her affection. And by making John the bad guy and herself the victim, she excused herself of any wrongdoing. There was little communication over the years and their children hardly knew each other. Today, thankfully, there has been somewhat of a reconciliation, but Betty has had a difficult time releasing her bitterness and resentment.

How did Betty, a Christian, get to this point? Because she believed Satan's lies and told herself, *John is Mr. Everything at school and I'm invisible. It's not fair because my grades are much better than his, and I'm a nicer person, but no one knows. Even Mom and Dad love him more. He gets the attention; he gets to use their car; his room is bigger than mine. I want to be as popular and as loved as John, but I must not be good enough. It's his fault. I'll punish him, and I'll punish Mom because I know John is her favorite. I won't love him. In fact, I'm going to pretend he doesn't exist. That's the only way I can bear the pain of being less worthy than John.*

What a poignant reminder to parents that comparing our children and having favorites is hurtful and unwise. Siblings naturally compare themselves to each other, but parents should make a point *not* to do so.

3. Incomplete Knowledge = Unfair Comparisons. Comparisons often lead to jealousy and envy because they are never really fair. When we weigh ourselves against others, we use limited and incomplete knowledge. Oh, we know ourselves well. We see the good, the bad, and the ugly. And, for some reason, we tend to minimize the good and maximize the bad. But when we look at others, all we see are the other person's good points. We tend *not* to see their faults and shortcomings or their problems and challenges.

Many single women envy my friend Michelle. They see that she is successful, travels the world, and wears gorgeous clothes and jewelry. But they don't see behind the scenes, where Michelle labors day after day, under the gun to make her writing deadlines. They don't see her alone in her motel room in some Podunk town almost every weekend or sit with her for hours in boring airports. If we knew the whole story about those we compare ourselves to, we might not envy them at all.

4. The need to win. Jealousy also flows out of our need to win. We are driven to be better than others because we think winning will make us worthy, loved, and valued. We live in a competitive society.

From the time our children are toddlers, they are involved in sports, and by the time they are in Little League, the competition is extreme. Coaches drive the children too hard and parents fight among themselves. All because we are so driven to *win*.

The desire to win is not a sin—unless we allow it to become the motivating factor in our lives and use inappropriate means to succeed. Remember the appalling news story of the mother who took out a contract on a teen's life because she wanted her daughter to get the cheerleader spot? Yes, this was an extreme case, but it illustrates the almost bloodthirsty intensity of competition.

This attitude flows over into our churches and ministries. Reverend Jack Frost tells the story of how his dad compared him and his brother. His dad was a professional tennis player and passionate about his sons' athletic abilities. Jack's brother was a strong tennis player, but Jack wasn't. He tells of playing tennis with his father and hearing him say, "No son of mine hits a net ball. Be a monster! Hit it harder." Of course, the pressure that put on Jack almost always resulted in his hitting a net ball. The look of loathing his father would give him after about three failures has stuck with him most of his life.

As Jack grew up and went into the ministry, that desperate need to perform and please followed him into the churches he pastored. He built large, thriving churches. He was reading his Bible through two and three times a year. He was getting up very early to spend time in personal devotions. He was doing everything right (or so he thought). But his wife was in a deep depression and his children were just as fearful of him as Jack had been of *his* father.

He was freed from this bondage only when he became aware of God's love. Jack realized his heavenly Father wasn't comparing him to his brother or anyone else. He didn't have to be the best to earn God's love. He didn't have to compete with other pastors.

It was the same in Paul's day. Some of the ministers in the city of Corinth were boasting in their accomplishments. Paul admonished the others not to compare themselves to those who were blowing their own horns. He told them not to measure their deeds by what others have done, but to focus on being obedient and pleasing the Lord (2 Corinthians 10:12-17). Paul understood that keeping score almost always leads to jealousy and envy rather than the perceived payoff of making us feel better about ourselves.

Please understand. There's nothing wrong with wanting to be better than we are. To sell more books. To grow your talents and abilities. To rise higher. My television program *Aspiring Women* is all about women aspiring to be their best. So what's the problem? Nothing, as long as our motives are pure and we keep the temptation of unhealthy comparison in check so that it does not result in jealousy, envy, or greed.

Recognizing the Green-Eyed Monster

How do you know when you've crossed over the line and succumbed to the temptation of unhealthy comparisons that lead to envy and jealousy? Here are some red flags that indicate a problem in this area.

- Do I feel pain because of another person's success?
- Do I feel that I deserve what I envy?
- Do I find myself wanting to put down successful people by gossiping about them or hurting them?
- Do I avoid seeing other people's successes?
- Do I find myself wanting to gain from other people's losses?
- Do I feel frustrated or irritable around a person, but can't figure out why?
- Do I attach a subtle put-down to compliments I give?
- Do I try to minimize or neutralize another's success?

Another fruit of inappropriate comparison is dissatisfaction, which is also a characteristic of greed.

Dissatisfaction

While it is possible to be dissatisfied with your current circumstances without it escalating into jealousy or envy, that is the usual progression. It is also possible to be satisfied with your circumstances or possessions, and so on, and to *still* battle jealousy.

During one of our television programs, we surveyed the audience about their most difficult issues. I was surprised that in this room of fifty young, successful-looking women, the biggest issue was *disappointment*. These women were not bedraggled or poor or uneducated. Yet, they struggled with disappointment over a number of issues. I had to ask, "What are they disappointed about and why?"

That eye-opening survey prompted the *Aspiring Women* team to do a more thorough questionnaire on our website. At the time of this writing, we have received nearly 1,000 responses to our "20 Good Questions." The survey helped us learn a lot about women's needs and where they're coming from.

One question was "What is the greatest problem in your marriage?" Unmet needs or expectations—*disappointment*—was the second most common answer. We often have expectations that exceed our real lives. Where do these unrealistic expectations come from? I believe they often spring from inappropriate comparisons. We see what other people have and it makes us discontent with what *we* have—it's the classic "Greener Grass Syndrome."

Many women in this country have succumbed to dissatisfaction. We have been so blessed with freedom and material possessions. Yet true contentment often eludes us. A trip overseas (like my visit with Tudor and Mirela) can cause us to realize how privileged we are and put our dissatisfaction and disappointment in perspective. As the apostle Paul pointed out, we can be content in almost any situation (Philippians 4:11).

However, our comparisons and accompanying disappointment often go beyond dishes and jewelry and houses. Have you ever been guilty of comparing your husband to other men? Don't fall into the trap of seeing all the good in other women's husbands and only the bad in your own mate.

You may be impressed by the way your friend's husband vacuums the rug for her or regularly cleans the kitchen. But perhaps what you don't know is he is so tight-fisted with money that he squeaks when he walks. Maybe your friend's husband never leaves his dirty clothes and shoes lying around like yours does, but he is so controlling in his neatness, he makes his wife miserable. While it may be tempting to compare your marriage and mate with those of your friends, don't succumb to this temptation. Here again, the comparisons are not fair and we use incomplete knowledge. It can ruin relationships and create unsettling discontentment.

Why do we fall prey to comparison that leads to dissatisfaction? The Eve Factor. Just like Eve, we believe the lies of the Enemy. When we're single we think we would be happy if only we could find a husband to meet all our needs. When we're married we think we would be happy if only we could have a child. And when we have children, we think things will be great once we get past the diapers. When our kids are older we think, *If only I can survive the teen years, things will be better.* Then we think, *If my husband just gets that promotion, money won't be such a problem, and then I'll be content.* Our satisfaction and happiness are elusive because of unrealistic expectations and because we don't understand that true contentment and joy don't come through externals.

We also fall prey to disappointment because we believe the lie that we need to have more. As I said earlier, it's admirable to try to make things better — your marriage, your appearance, your home, your job. As is often the case, the lie has an element of truth. God wants us to be our best. He wants us to keep growing. *But not at the cost of being dissatisfied with where we are right now.*

True peace and contentment does not depend on your being the biggest or best. It depends on a close relationship with Christ and resting in His love.

As destructive as jealousy, envy, greed and dissatisfaction are, the most devastating fruit of inappropriate comparison may be that it *feeds* a woman's lack of self-esteem.

Low Self-Esteem

Though low self-esteem is not a sin, I bring it up here because this weakness can lead to jealousy, envy, dissatisfaction, and other self-destructive behaviors. It is one of the deadly fruits of comparison.

As a part of our Internet survey, we asked women what held them back from achieving their goals. Their number two answer was lack of confidence or self-image. Even more revealing was what women named as their most difficult emotion to deal with—feelings of rejection. A close second was fear and anxiety.

More of a Problem for Women

Later in the book I discuss the temptation of pride and self-sufficiency, but pride seems to be more of a problem for men than for women. Mary Ellen Ashcroft is a teacher and writer who has unusual insight into the challenges women face. She shares some poignant quotes about this interesting distinction between men and women:

> Many women do not suffer from too much self-confidence but from self-hatred; this fact is born out by psychologists, sociologists, and literary historians. For instance, when women write autobiographies they write them very differently from

men. Women who write autobiographies have usually been highly successful in some way, but they apologize about their deficiencies and try to explain.[2]

To be sure, it is usually said that sin in its original form is man's wanting to be as God. But that is only the one side of sin. The other side of such pride is hopelessness, resignation, inertia and melancholy. . . . Temptation consists not so much in the titanic desire to be as God, but in weakness, timidity, weariness . . .[3]

Does that hit too close to home with you? I was appalled as I read what some women have written about themselves.

There are times when I look in the mirror and want to smash it. Lots of times I feel I'm not worth walking out the door. I see myself as a really useless, small and pathetic person, basically a piece of dirt.[4]

I guess the feeling I most often have toward myself is this nagging loathing, a kind of disgust. Sometimes everything about me, especially my body, seems disgusting. Then I get even more disgusted with myself for being filled with this self-disgust.[5]

Understanding Why

Where does this self-hatred come from? Why is crippling inferiority so prevalent in women? There are many causes. Jennifer O'Neill, who I talked about in chapter one, felt inferior because her parents were so caught up in their relationship, they ignored her. I struggled with this because I wasn't affirmed and was made to feel incompetent.

Another serious contributor—one over which we have some control—is our propensity to compare ourselves with others, and then allow our magnified shortcomings to make us feel even worse about ourselves. Add to that the competition and pressure put on women today to be a supermom, have a successful career, keep a perfect home, exercise and eat right, be active in church, and spend quality time with God. It's just too much; none of us can do it all.

But we believe the lie that other women *are* doing it all. We believe we should look like the touched-up photos of models on magazine covers. We believe our forty-year-old bodies should look like the firm, petite twenty-one-year-old bodies in spandex at the health club. We beat ourselves up and sink into depression.

I am convinced the most imposing barrier to a woman's success, fulfillment, and a purpose-filled life is a negative view of herself—which is fueled by inappropriate comparison. We are surrounded by those more beautiful, gifted, affluent, and talented than we are. And if we indulge in comparing ourselves with them, we will begin to feel inferior—even if we didn't before!

The Dangers of Low Self-Esteem

The woman with low self-esteem is in danger of yielding to a variety of temptations. Her insecurity can drive her to search for love and affirmation from the wrong sources. Sanguines are particularly vulnerable to unhealthy comparisons because one of our greatest needs is for acceptance and approval. We notice every detail of others we admire, are more tuned in to differences, and are thus more apt to fall into destructive comparing.

All women who struggle with low self-esteem must be on guard when it comes to sexual temptation. We want desperately to be appreciated, loved, and cherished. If we are not finding affirmation through our husbands, we may unconsciously look for it elsewhere.

Women with low self-esteem are also susceptible to the temptation to overspend. Have you ever considered yourself a shopaholic? I love to shop for clothes and have a full closet to prove it. I have often justified my shopping habit by reminding myself that I only purchase clearance and sale items. But I have come to see that my shopping and occasional overspending gives me a high—an adrenaline rush, a temporary fix—when I am feeling low. Have you ever gone shopping because you needed cheering up? It works—for a while. But purchases don't satisfy very long.

Some women believe they will be loved if they are slim, so they purge or starve themselves to lose weight, hoping to find acceptance. Instead, their pain and dysfunction can grow more serious, threatening to destroy their health or even their lives. The urge to find satisfaction *and self-worth* in a new outfit, new sofa, new car, or a new body draws us every time.

If you struggle with self-hatred, you are right where Satan wants you. He wants you to judge yourself harshly, and he wants to keep you inferior, unlovable, and unworthy. But there are some things you can do to bolster your self-esteem and thus increase your ability to stand strong against the temptation of unhealthy comparison.

Build Your Resistance

How can you resist the snares of comparison, jealousy, envy, dissatisfaction, and greed? None of us *wants* to be envious or jealous, yet most of us are envious at one time or another. What can you do to build your resistance so that you don't fall prey to the sins that result from unhealthy comparisons?

Develop a Healthy Self-Love

When you look in the mirror, do you like what you see? Appropriate self-love can help you be less susceptible to many temptations. The

Bible advocates that we have a *healthy* self-love, which is not arrogance or lack of humility. For women who have years of hurt or major challenges to their self-confidence, this is obviously much easier said than done. But it is completely possible. You can learn just how valuable and special you are in God's eyes.

Regardless of how you view yourself, God loves you unconditionally and sees your potential. Even when you are living as you please, without a single thought for God, He still loves you (Romans 5:7-8). Here are some ideas for how to develop a healthy self-love:

- Become familiar with the hundreds of promises in the Bible. Find a book of Bible promises such as *The Bible Promise Book* (Barbour Publishing, Inc.) or *All the Promises of the Bible* (Zondervan). Here are a few references to get you started. Psalms 46:1-3; 37:24; 55:22; Job 8:21; Nahum 1:7; Jeremiah 29:11; John 16:33.
- Read the Psalms every day.
- Surround yourself with affirming, encouraging friends. Some people, without realizing it, demean others and feed a poor self-image. Get these women (or men) out of your life.
- Discipline yourself to focus on your strengths and submit your weaknesses to God.
- Ask Him to give you a healthy view of yourself.
- Remember that your true value was demonstrated by Christ's death on the cross.

When you feel better about yourself and understand your importance to God, you can then feel confident enough to be honest about your sin and move forward to overcome it. The first step is to examine your life for any sign of jealousy, envy, or dissatisfaction. Then admit it and ask forgiveness.

Recognize and Repent

Ask yourself the questions listed in the sidebar on page 63, "Recognizing the Green-Eyed Monster." Be brutally honest with yourself and God. Don't try to rationalize your inappropriate feelings toward others. Call them what they are.

Once you are aware of any jealousy or envy, repent. Even if the inappropriate feelings have crept into your heart without your realizing it, ask for God's forgiveness and help to be rid of the sin. You may also need to ask forgiveness from the person you feel envy or jealousy toward. Since envy is a secret sin, it may be better to keep it a secret. But if your envy or jealousy has resulted in gossip, or if you have hurt someone through spiteful behavior, a sincere apology is definitely called for. If your jealousy is the result of greed or destructive competition, a selfish need to win, you must pray for forgiveness and deliverance.

Learn from Your Envy

Examine what it is that's creating your envy or jealousy. We can't help it if we see something we want. But we can determine *why* we want it so much. Is it because we feel that a *thing* will give us self-worth? Is it because we crave acceptance and think acquiring it will make others love us? Or could it be we just want to improve ourselves?

For example, let's say you can't help wanting to be like your friend Kathleen. She is always so put together. You know she doesn't spend a lot of money on clothes, but she always looks fantastic. She just has a knack for putting outfits together. No matter how hard you try, you always feel a bit frumpy. It's just not your gift. Kathleen is great with her makeup, too. It's stunning without being overdone—while you've never really learned how to use makeup. Every time you see Kathleen, you envy her sophisticated image. How can you keep your admiration and envy from turning into jealousy?

Why not talk to Kathleen and tell her how much you like the way she wears her clothes and makeup? Ask her if she would be willing to help you. She might even go shopping with you and make suggestions on purchases and help you with simple makeup techniques. Chances are she will be thrilled; imitation is the greatest compliment. But if you don't feel comfortable with that, find a department store or beauty salon to consult with you, and actively work on improving your appearance so you'll feel better about yourself. Learn from your envy and let it make you better, but don't let it turn into sin.

Pray About Your Needs and Wants

"So let us come boldly to the very throne of God and stay there to receive his mercy and to find grace to help us in our times of need" (Hebrews 4:16, TLB). Ask God to purify your motives and reveal any wrong attitudes; then talk to Him about what it is you want. The Bible tells us God loves to give us the *desires of our heart* (Psalm 37:4). He will not honor greed or materialism, but He certainly understands our need for earthly as well as spiritual provision.

Remember, Jesus' first miracle was to turn water into wine at a wedding party. His mother understood the colossal embarrassment it was to run short of wine and didn't hesitate to ask her son to intervene. We women have been calling on the Lord's help in similar situations ever since, and He is faithful to provide for our needs and often our desires.

Submit to God's Plan for Your Life *at This Time*

Realize that each woman is at a different place and has a different calling. God showed me I could get rid of my jealousy when I embraced His will for *me* and relinquished my own plans and ambitions. I came to the place where I could be content with the ministry God had given me *for this season of my life*. God showed me that my self-worth and success don't depend on how many books I sell or how many conferences I speak at. Although Tammy, Michelle, and I have a lot in common, we are not at the same place. I have another full-time job besides my speaking and writing. I have grandchildren that I am committed to pouring my life into, which takes time. My television show touches thousands of women and must be a priority. And my talent and ability may never provide the same opportunities that Tammy and Michelle enjoy. But God showed me I absolutely cannot fall into the trap of comparing myself with others. That knowledge has freed me to bask in the dear friendship of my cohosts, to sincerely rejoice in and celebrate their successes, and to be grateful for my own opportunities. I learned a lot about myself through my jealousy.

Determine the Cause of Your Dissatisfaction

If you struggle with disappointment or dissatisfaction, verbalize or even write down what is missing from your life that is stealing your peace. Determine *why* you are discontent. Have unhealthy comparisons made you feel relative deprivation? Have you compared your husband or boyfriend to other men and become dissatisfied with your relationship? Do you have unrealistic expectations from others or yourself? Pinpoint where your disappointment is coming from. Some women have a niggling sense of disappointment without knowing why. With others, the disappointment has a face and a name. There may be things you can do to make your marriage (or whatever you are disappointed about) improve. If not, give it to God, get over it, and don't let it feed your dissatisfaction.

Practice the Art of Thankfulness and Gratitude

Those of us who are greatly blessed (and most American women are) often become so egocentric, we don't see the neediness of those around us. As I mentioned earlier, a trip overseas or a day volunteering in a soup kitchen might change your perspective.

I recently interviewed a female prisoner. I have on several occasions spoken to incarcerated women, but I had never before taken cameras into a prison for a story about an inmate. Theresa has been in jail for nineteen years. She hopes to get released next year, but may have to serve ten more years. She came to Christ shortly after her arrest and during the past nineteen years she has graduated from Bible school, written a book, and established a not-for-profit ministry—all from behind bars. When I asked her about her ministry to the homeless, she made this amazing state-ment: "I want to help the homeless because I realize I am so much more fortunate than they are. I have a warm place to sleep and food to eat. They don't."

Wow! Here is a woman who could compare herself to others and be dissatisfied. Yet she has a joy, peace, and serenity that blew my mind. Theresa has cultivated a thankful heart in spite of her circumstances. She reminds me of a woman of the Bible who also resisted the temptation to compare and be dissatisfied.

FINDING TRUE CONTENTMENT

This woman of the Old Testament resisted temptation and demon-strated some remarkable qualities that we can admire and emulate. The writer of 2 Kings doesn't give her name, but I've called her Shunami because she lived near Shunem.

Shunami was a woman of considerable means, well known, and respected by her neighbors. She was gracious and hospitable. But Shunami had another quality that is even more noteworthy.

Shunami and her husband developed a close friendship with the prophet Elisha through inviting him into their home whenever he came to their area. The couple received much more than they gave because, though they lived in a godless culture, Elisha introduced them to the one true God.

His visits became so regular that Shunami decided to take her hospitality to another level. She prepared a guest room for him on the roof of her home. She furnished it simply, but adequately, and it became a great blessing to the itinerant prophet.

Elisha was so appreciative of her kindness, he wanted to do something for her in return. A close friend of the king, Elisha was a powerful figure and could have rewarded her in a number of ways. But when he asked Shunami what she wanted, she said, "Nothing. I am perfectly content" (2 Kings 4:13, TLB).

She wanted nothing! She could have asked for wealth, status, lands, special favors, exemption from paying taxes, or all of the above. But she had been kind to the prophet through pure motives; she wanted nothing in return. She was perfectly content.

Yet, the prophet was determined to do something nice for her, and he saw that she was childless. This is significant, especially since she had just insisted she was content and didn't need anything. In those days it was considered a terrible disgrace to be barren, and Shunami could have easily resorted to whining and self-pity. And though she was well-off financially, her husband was an old man. Surely she must have been tempted to compare herself to all the women around her who had younger husbands and children. But instead of focusing on what she didn't have, Shunami focused on the blessings she had. Her childlessness had not made her bitter. She had not yielded to the temptation of envy, jealousy, or dissatisfaction. Elisha promised her a child, and the next year her son was born.

If an angel appeared at your door and offered to grant any request, what would your wish list look like? Perhaps you would be tempted to ask for material things. Or you might ask for a perfect husband who would make all your dreams come true. Maybe your request would be for your children or others. Or maybe you could declare like Shunami — *I am content.*

Shunami's Character Traits to Emulate:

- She gave generously to others without expecting reciprocation.
- She did not compare herself to others and become jealous.
- She did not allow her disappointment to make her bitter.
- She did not grasp at the opportunity to better herself.
- She was perfectly content.

It is important to strive for God's best and always keep growing, but not at the cost of never being satisfied where you are right now. Focus on God's blessings. Concentrate on what you *do* have, not what you *don't* have. And discover the elusive, but glorious freedom of true contentment.

The next time you are tempted to nibble on the apples of unhealthy comparison, envy, or jealousy, don't give in. Once you are aware of the danger, you can sidestep the pettiness, rise above the self-indulgence, and learn to be content with who you are in Christ. Compare yourself only to yourself and the standard God has laid forth in His Word. Realize that God doesn't compare you with anyone. Aren't you glad? But instead He loves us individually, and He patiently leads us toward His ultimate plan and purpose.

CHAPTER THREE:
GREENER GRASS, GREED,
AND THE GREEN-EYED MONSTER

Study and Explore

Read what the Bible says about envy, and write down what you learn. If a consequence is given, be sure to write it down. (Remember envy is also called covetousness).

Example: Job 5:2 — It slays the simple.
Proverbs 23:17
Mark 7:21-23
Luke 12:15
Romans 1:29-32
Romans 13:13
Galatians 5:21
Colossians 3:5-6
Hebrews 13:5
James 3:16

Now examine the Scriptures below to understand why Christians should be confident and feel valued and special. List the reason beside the Scripture. These are only a few examples of God's love for us.

Example: Psalm 139:14-16 — God knew us before we were born.
Matthew 10:39-41 If we recieve Him - He recieves us.
John 3:16 God loved us so much He gave up His Son
Hebrews 13:5 Never will He leave us - never to forsake
1 Peter 2:24 Thro Christ Jesus sacrifice o n the cross. us. Our sins will die and our wounds healed.

77

Consider and Reflect

1. Why do you think Paul considered it unwise to compare ourselves with others? (2 Corinthians 10:12-17)

2. What are some appropriate comparisons? How can they help us?

3. In Psalm 37:4 we are promised God will give us the desires of our heart, but what is the condition of that promise? Why is this condition attached?

4. Have you been guilty of comparing yourself with others and coming up on the short end? How have you compared your children or your husband with others? Though it is difficult to admit it, write down the names of the people involved in the comparisons.

5. If you have ever been envious or jealous of others, write down the names of those involved and name the thing you were envious of.

6. Think about why you wanted that thing so much. If you don't know, ask God to reveal your deep needs that made you envy what someone else has.

7. If you have ever gossiped about someone out of envy, or tried to hurt them or minimize their success, ask God to give you the courage and opportunity to ask them for forgiveness (if appropriate).

8. Have inappropriate comparisons caused dissatisfaction to creep into your life? Repent of the dissatisfaction and focus on your blessings. Write a list of your blessings and thank God for them.

9. Compare yourself to yourself one year ago. Write down the areas where you have grown. For example, parenting skills, relationship with your husband, time spent in prayer and devotions, and so on. Make note of the areas that need work. Ask God to help you.

10. When you look in the mirror do you like what you see? Write down a list of the things you like about yourself—your strengths and assets. On the other side of the paper write down the things you don't like—your weaknesses and flaws. Chances are the negative list will be longer. Now ask God to change the flaws that can be changed and to help you accept those that cannot be changed. Realize that your limitations give God a chance to be glorified.

Pray

Lord Jesus, forgive me for falling into the trap of inappropriate comparisons. I repent of my envy, jealousy, and discontentment. Help me to fully realize my worth and value in Your eyes. Give me confidence and a healthy self-image based on Your great love for me that was demonstrated by Your death on the cross. Help me to grow closer to You and be my best for Your glory. Teach me true humility and help me to focus on others before myself. In Your name I pray, Amen.

OUT OF YOUR COMFORT ZONE AND INTO SIGNIFICANCE

The Temptation of Complacency

A Christian never falls asleep in the fire, or in deep waters,
but he is likely to grow drowsy in the sunshine.

W. G. BURNS

My husband and I don't have a lot of hobbies in common. Jerry plays golf; I've tried twice and we both agreed it was hopeless. He's a sailor; I'm afraid of the water. He is a horse person; I'm not. He grew up in Texas around quarter horses and rodeos. When my daughter, at age eight, decided she wanted to ride, Jerry was thrilled. Vanessa began riding lessons at a nearby stable and took to it like a duck to water. She was a natural equestrian, and it turned out to be a wonderful hobby for both of them.

I, on the other hand, grew up near a large city and was never around horses. I don't like dust, hay, spiders, manure, or much contact with an animal too large to pick up and cuddle. Since it worked out well for Jerry and Vanessa to have this time together, I never made an effort to be a part of that world.

When Vanessa grew up and had children of her own, she and her husband bought a small farm and had several horses. My granddaughters also loved them and took riding lessons at a young age. Jerry was at their farm every Saturday, playing the cowboy.

I finally realized if I were going to be an integral part of something my family loved, I needed to learn to ride horses and how to be safe around them. So at an appalling age (far past my fiftieth birthday), I began taking horseback riding lessons. To my amazement, I thoroughly enjoyed it. I wasn't the best student, but I progressed slowly and learned both English and Western techniques.

I had been riding for almost two years, when during a lesson, my sweet, gentle gelding decided to start bucking. He catapulted me into the air, landing me on my head and shoulder. I sustained some significant and painful injuries to my shoulder and knee.

After six weeks of physical therapy and several months of recovery, I did, in fact, begin riding again. I needed to prove to myself I could get back in the saddle. But after a while, I realized horseback riding was not something I loved and decided I wasn't going to take the risk of riding every week.

I entered the world of horses for my husband and my grandchildren (and myself too) and the rewards were many. I can go trail riding with Jerry if I want. I conquered something athletic, which gave me a lot of personal satisfaction and a sense of accomplishment. (And it was much easier than golf!) I don't think anything I've ever done has brought me closer to my husband.

But I also learned firsthand that getting out of our comfort zone and taking risks is just that—a risk. Sometimes we get hurt, embarrassed, or misunderstood, and we can fall flat on our faces in failure. But that doesn't mean we should give in to complacency. No risk we take is as dangerous as the temptation to sit on the sidelines of life and do nothing.

A DEFINITION

What is *complacency*? It's "self-satisfaction, contentment to the point of inactivity, smugness, or self-righteousness." Complacency or indifference is the tendency to stay in our comfort zone. It's choosing to do the *safe* thing or nothing at all.

Pastor and writer Rick Ezell describes indifference or complacency as *sloth*, one of the seven deadly sins. His description leaves me cold, but captures the essence of this unattractive quality at its worst:

> We might call it laziness, apathy, tolerance, or despair. Whatever we call it, it is the sin that believes in nothing, cares for nothing, seeks to know nothing, interferes with nothing, enjoys nothing, loves nothing, hates nothing, finds purpose in nothing, and lives for nothing, and it remains alive only because it would die for nothing. It forever remains on the sidelines, unmoved, uncaring, uninvolved.[1]

I don't know about you, but I don't want to live my life that way. Yet most of us have given in to the temptation of complacency at one time or another.

Have you ever felt stuck in a rut? You know you should be doing more than you are, but you just don't have the energy or motivation. You're not happy with your weight, but can't seem to stick to your diet or exercise. You feel sorry for others less fortunate, but never get around to doing anything to help. You know you should be sharing your faith, but fear holds you back. You see your relationship with your husband declining, but it's too much work to try and fix it. You're bored, but figure boredom is better than the unknown, so you keep doing the same things over and over. Besides, you are just too tired most of the time to want any drama in your life. If you have felt any of the above, you've experienced complacency.

Guess which personality type is most vulnerable to complacency. Yep—the Phlegmatic. You laid-back, peaceful stabilizers of the world must beware of this temptation. But so must the rest of us. It's human nature to take the course of least resistance, and we all deal with fear of taking risks, lack of confidence, boredom, indifference, or just plain laziness.

We tend to think of temptation and the sin that follows as something we *do,* but it can also be something we *fail* to do. We can become comfortable, so unwilling to put forth any effort that we miss the greatest opportunities for ministry and blessing. We tell ourselves we are fine right where we are. We are okay. God is happy; we're happy. We don't have to do anything. But don't you believe it; those are Satan's lies!

Let's look at some of the various fruits of complacency so you can recognize it when it slips into your life.

HOW ARE WE TEMPTED TO BE COMPLACENT?

If any of the following ring true for you, it's likely that you are vulnerable to this temptation and have yielded to it.

Failure to Grow Our Relationship with God

A. W. Tozer said, "Contentment with earthly goods is the mark of a saint; contentment with our spiritual state is a mark of inward blindness. One of the greatest foes of the Christian is religious complacency."[2] Our Christian walk is the one area where we should *never* stop striving. Our relationship with Christ, like any other relationship, takes work, and if we don't grow, we regress.

Spiritual complacency is a hidden sin that can bring coldness where the fires of commitment once burned. It robs us of fellowship and intimacy with Jesus. That's why complacency is such a tool in Satan's hands. He knows we don't have to commit some grievous sin when complacency will do the job nicely.

Failure to Live as Though Jesus Is Returning

Perhaps the greatest danger of complacency is the possibility of missing the Lord's return.

> Watch out! Don't let my sudden coming catch you unawares; don't let me find you living in careless ease. (Luke 21:34, TLB)

> So be prepared, for you don't know what day your Lord is coming. (Matthew 24:42, TLB)

If you are a wife or mother, your life may consist of doing many of the same things over and over again. Don't allow yourself to become anesthetized by the comfort and routine of your day-to-day existence. Keep clearly in mind the fleeting nature of this life and the urgency of making every moment count for eternity.

Failure to Obey God's Leading

In the early seventies my husband managed a Christian television network in Dallas for Pat Robertson. Jerry had felt called to Christian broadcasting for several years, and God had finally opened the door. Jerry loved what he did. He often cohosted the *700 Club* with Pat. Dallas was great; we had close friends; it was Jerry's hometown. Life was good.

After a couple of years Pat asked Jerry to come to Portsmouth, Virginia, to be operations manager of the network. Jerry told him we would pray about it, but everything in us resisted the idea. We felt like Virginia was *the North*. We knew no one in Portsmouth, and the job description sounded ambiguous. We were just not ready to make a move.

One day Jerry walked into his office and picked up the phone to make a call. He realized he couldn't see the numbers on the dial. His head was pounding. He discovered he couldn't speak properly and had numbness in one side of his body. An electroencephalogram (EEG) revealed an abnormality in the left side of his brain, which was diagnosed as a brain tumor.

There is not room here to tell the complete story of Jerry's journey of panic, then supernatural peace, and finally a complete and miraculous healing.[3] But this experience taught us that staying in the center of God's will is more important than homes or friends or what town you live in. Jerry told me, "We'll be vagabonds for God for the rest of our lives if that's what He wants." In just a few months we had moved to Virginia.

Did God allow Jerry's illness in order to shake us out of our lethargy? We think He did. We yielded to the temptation of complacency when we resisted the idea of moving because we were too comfortable where we were. We did not actively seek God's will about what *He* wanted. God certainly got our attention. But deep in our hearts we already knew He was prompting us to make a change. What would the fallout have been if we had refused to obey? God may still have given us a chance to pursue our calling, but I believe we would have missed God's best.

Move when it's time to move, obey when God is speaking, and never get so comfortable you give in to complacency.

Allow Your Blessings to Become a Curse

The more blessings we have, the more vulnerable we are to the temptation of spiritual complacency. When things are going well, our prayer life gets sporadic. When the pantry is full of food, the bank account has a healthy balance, and the kids are doing well in school, our devotional life takes second or third place. God becomes distant and church attendance becomes routine or something we do only out of a sense of duty. Spiritual indifference pushes our spiritual lives to the back burner. When this happens our blessings have become a curse.

On the other hand, when someone we love gets a frightening diagnosis or tragedy strikes our family, spiritual complacency becomes spiritual *intensity* overnight. We suddenly become serious about God when our blessings are taken away. Could this be one of the reasons God allows bad things to happen to good people? I believe it is.

Failure to Reach Out to Others

There was a time when neighbors in rural areas needed each other. People needed help to build their houses and barns, help to gather their crops, help when their babies were born. But today people can be very self-sufficient. We avoid reaching out to others and building strong friendships. Many of us don't know our neighbors and don't care to. It takes effort, time, and self-sacrifice to get involved with others' lives.

Remember the story of the Good Samaritan in Luke 10? An innocent traveler was attacked by thieves and left for dead. The first person to notice the injured man was a priest. He was a servant of God who should have had compassion for the poor fellow. But when he saw the man, he crossed over to the other side of the road and kept on walking. The next person to come by was a Levite — also a religious man. The Levite walked over and evaluated the situation, then he too made the decision to do nothing.

Finally, a despised Samaritan came along. When he saw the injured man, he felt sorry for him, cared for his wounds, put him on his own donkey, took him to an inn, and paid for his care. Though the

Samaritan was considered a third- or fourth-class citizen, he was the one who showed mercy. Jesus said, "Go and do likewise" (verse 37).

The two religious men refused to leave their comfort zone, even when confronted with dire need and human suffering. In a similar way, we sit in church and don't even greet those next to us. They could be in pain but we never know. How smug and self-righteous we can become as we hurry about our religious activities—often missing genuine opportunities to share Christ's love with those in need all around us.

We must guard against the temptation of complacency when it comes to witnessing and sharing our faith with others. We must be willing to tell others about God and our faith. It takes time and effort to build friendships and enlarge our circle of influence, but that's the best way to share our faith. Our homes are valuable tools in reaching out to others, yet hospitality is a lost art.

Failure to Speak Up or Bring About Change

Silence can be another fruit of complacency. I have met several women who were being abused by their husbands, yet these women continued in the situation for years. How can women be so complacent in a horrible situation? Here is where The Eve Factor takes over in a radical way, because they choose to believe a lie.

Many abused women believe their husbands or boyfriends will improve. They remain in a bad situation because they are afraid of change—afraid the future might be worse than what they are dealing with now. They fear their children will starve or go without, or they fear what their husband will do if they make him angry by refusing to put up with the abuse. Other women fail to speak up when they are unhappy in their marriage because their husband is overly controlling or emotionally distant from them or their children.

Don't let complacency keep you silent when you should speak up and *do* something.

Take Your Husband and Marriage for Granted

Complacency in marriage may be the biggest factor in divorce.

Ray and Anita had one of the strongest marriages of any couple I knew. Both outdoor types, they loved raising animals and gardening. They had much in common. Both were musical, and they led worship and worked on choral and dramatic productions together. The two were inseparable.

They moved to California when Ray felt God wanted him to pursue his master's degree in choral conducting. He took a part-time position as music director of a church while he continued his education. The move brought increased expenses and decreased income, so Anita had no choice but to get a full-time job outside the home. She had a long commute on the freeways and little time for the church activities. She still sang in the choir, but that was about all.

Ray eventually became the music minister at a large, successful church and became even more absorbed with his ministry. Anita was supportive, but again pulled back her own involvement. She still had one teenager at home, a demanding job, and the stressful freeway commute left her exhausted. She felt she didn't even have time for friendships.

I couldn't have been more shocked when I received a call one day from Anita. She was in tears and told me her life was falling apart. "What's wrong?" I asked. "Is it the children or your parents?"

"No," sobbed my friend. "It's my marriage. Ray has resigned his position at the church, and we're getting a divorce."

I couldn't believe it. Not Ray and Anita! My mind grasped at the possibilities. Maybe Ray had, in a moment of weakness, had a moral indiscretion with a choir member. But there was no other woman. There were no problems with money or the children. Ray and Anita had simply drifted apart.

The estrangement didn't happen overnight. There was nothing either of them had done to cause the problem. It was what they *hadn't done*. Ray needed affirmation and acceptance from his wife, but seldom felt she gave it. He tried to tell her on a number of occasions, but she wasn't listening. Anita felt she was a victim in a situation beyond her control. She had been handed a situation she didn't want or like. But instead of speaking up and insisting they work to find a better solution, Anita continued to withdraw from Ray's activities and his life. Anita took the course of least resistance. She fell into the trap of thinking that because the situation was not her doing, she didn't have to try to correct it. They continued to drift apart until Ray finally dropped the bomb that he didn't want to be married anymore. He didn't want to be a pastor anymore. He saw no other solution but to end his ministry and his marriage.

I'm thankful to report that Ray and Anita did *not* get that divorce. They decided as a last-ditch effort to attend *Cleansing Stream* at Jack Hayford's church. This restorative, inner-healing ministry not only saved their marriage, but Ray and Anita began their own ministry to be a resource for pastors who want to include *Cleansing Stream* in their own churches. Their relationship today is better than ever. Having just celebrated their fortieth anniversary, they are best friends and have a strong marriage. But they admit that complacency almost destroyed their relationship.

Don't be so naïve as to think you can just let your marriage happen. It's much the same as your relationship with God. There's no such thing as coasting.

I believe those of us who hold our marriage vows sacred could be even more vulnerable to complacency in marriage. Because we don't believe in divorce, many of us settle for mediocre marriages rather than working to improve them. We stay together for convenience or for the sake of the children. We think our marriage is immune to infidelity and adultery, and that because our husband is a Christian, he will always be around. Statistics prove us wrong.

I recently talked with a clinical psychologist who specializes in working with troubled couples. He said, "The biggest enemy of a *great* marriage is a *good* marriage." I don't want complacency to steal the gusto from any part of my life—especially my marriage.

Neglect Your Health and Appearance

Do you hate high school reunions as much as I do? It's so uncomfortable seeing how much everyone's appearance has changed. The guys are bald and the women are fat. We shake our heads and think, *Boy, she really let herself go!*

I'm joking, of course. Many people in my high school class still look great. But the difference between those who have aged well after twenty-five years and those who haven't could be complacency. Many women who are diligent about their relationship with God and take good care of others are appallingly indifferent about attention to themselves.

These have fallen for the lie that it is more important to take care of our families than to take care of ourselves, and that it makes us more *spiritual* to deny ourselves. We believe if we take time for ourselves, we are being selfish. Those of us who struggle with a poor self-image believe deep down that we are not worthy of such time and effort, so it's easy to yield to the temptation of complacency in our appearance and health.

Is appearance really that important? Is it something God is concerned about? Absolutely! Even some young women let their physical appearance decline shamefully. I know our looks are partly due to our gene pool, but there is no excuse for not trying to look our best.

The temptation of complacency is one of the hardest to recognize and resist because it doesn't come through inappropriate *action*. It is subtle and creeps in slowly through *inaction* as we go about our daily lives. However, there are some proactive ways you can avoid it.

Build Your Resistance

The following suggestions can help you build your resistance to complacency. Notice they all require intentional effort and ACTION! These important life changes will happen because you *make them happen.*

Grow Your Relationship with God

In order to avoid spiritual complacency, you must regularly take stock in your relationship with God. Do you feel closer to the Lord than you did last year or last month? Is it more difficult for you to make time for personal devotions; do you easily find excuses for skipping your quiet time? Do you enjoy church or endure it?

If you are a Phlegmatic or feel that you are susceptible to spiritual lethargy, you need to be especially disciplined in faith-building activities. Bible study, prayer, meditation, attending church, private worship, and involvement with other Christians cannot be an option. Write it in your calendar if necessary. Attend Bible studies with another woman or with your husband and hold each other accountable.

Try to cultivate a heavenly perspective instead of an earthly one. "Set your minds on things above, not on earthly things" (Colossians 3:2). Remind yourself regularly that Christ is returning and that this present world is only temporary. Remember that the most important priority in life is to love God and be obedient to His will.

We must also train our ears to pick out God's voice in the midst of all the others shouting for our attention. Years ago Jerry trained to be a radioman in the U.S. Coast Guard. He would sit and watch the radioman receiving the messages aboard ship. All Jerry could hear was a confusing cacophony of sounds coming through the receiver. There were several different Morse Code messages, voices, and considerable static coming through at the same time. But the radioman would calmly sit and type out the correct message for his ship. When Jerry asked him how he was able to determine the right one he said, "Because I have a trained ear."

Your relationship with God will grow as you learn to recognize the voice of the Holy Spirit. The more we seek to recognize God's voice and His leading, the more trained our ears become. There is the voice of common reason—not always in line with what God wants for us. There is the voice of friends and family. There is the voice of the Enemy, who wants to bring confusion. Then there is the voice of complacency that says, *Don't take the risk.*

Most people never hear the audible voice of God, but He has ways of speaking and making His wishes known. Learn to recognize His voice by praying about every decision, and then *expecting* His direction and listening for it. He can put an impression or "urging" in your mind or the Holy Spirit may speak to you through Scripture.

If you truly desire God's will for your life, He will make clear what He wants you to do.

Grow Your Relationships with Others, Especially Your Spouse

Other relationships take work too. Again, take stock. Do you have fewer friends than you used to? Do you feel more isolated? Don't let complacency rob you of the richness of close friends who can encourage you and hold you accountable. This is essential when it comes to resisting temptation, including the temptation of complacency!

What about your marriage? Do you feel closer to your husband than you did last year, or do you feel more distant? Do you communicate less? Have you let work crowd out your time together? Is there more friction between you? Be proactive. If your marriage is in trouble, speak up about it and get some help from your pastor or a Christian counselor. If your husband is abusive to you and your children, don't remain silent. Take the necessary steps to protect your kids and yourself.

If you are in a good marriage, don't allow it to decline. Try making it *great!* Spend quality time together every day—even if it's only fifteen minutes. Listen to your husband and make sure he listens to you. You may think sex equals intimacy, but it's not necessarily the same. You and your husband might be having sex, but drifting apart on a more important level. That deep soul connection can take place in other ways: touching or talking, baring your hearts to each other, sharing your innermost dreams with each other, and comforting and encouraging one another in times of stress or anxiety.

Then evaluate your sex life. I am amazed at how many women share with me that their sex life is nonexistent. Have you let busyness or your children or lethargy interfere with sex? Do you work at making your sex life exciting and look for ways of pleasing your husband? Complacency can do its work, even in this most important area of marriage.

And finally, keep talking about all aspects of your relationship. Keep the communication alive. Talk about where you are and what you both can do to make things better. Your husband may be uncomfortable with this kind of talk and any probing questions at first. But when he knows you only want to make things better, he will likely cooperate.

Don't Become Too Attached to Things

When our lives are full and carefree, we are more susceptible to complacency. So hold your material possessions and other blessings loosely. Don't allow your blessings to become a curse. When my husband got a promotion with Doubleday Broadcasting in the early years of his career, our family moved to El Paso, Texas. Jerry was happy to be moving into management and knew he needed the experience. However, he also knew God was calling him to be in full-time religious broadcasting eventually. We loved our life in El Paso. We lived in the nicest home we had ever had. Jerry was given a company vehicle—a flashy sports car. Working for the CBS station provided all kinds of trade-outs and perks. There were several restaurants where our family could eat free, because they advertised on that channel. We even got custom draperies for our home at no cost.

These kinds of arrangements are strictly legitimate and very common in commercial broadcasting. However, we were careful never to forget these blessings were temporary. We said many times during those two years, "We love our home and all the perks, but when God calls us into full-time Christian work, the 'For Sale' sign goes up." It wasn't easy to have that perspective, but we did not let our blessings become a curse. When Jerry was asked by Pat Robertson to take over the Christian station in another city, the "For Sale" sign went up and we moved.

We have never again had those kinds of perks, but God has still blessed us abundantly. If we had let our comfort and contentment in El Paso crowd out our willingness to obey God's voice, our complacency would have become sin.

Think Beyond Yourself and Reach Out to Others

Another safeguard for resisting complacency is reaching out to others in a structured way. I had the opportunity to teach a Bible study to a group of drug-addicted women who had checked themselves into a rehab center in inner-city Chicago. These women had more in common than their addictions. They were all pregnant. They wanted to get clean and sober and have drug-free, healthy babies.

As I met with these women each week, I took delight in describing God's unconditional love for them. I talked about Christ's death on the cross and explained salvation. I found that my teaching was really *pre-evangelism* because most of the women had no background in spiritual things or the Bible. I prayed with them about their problems, and many asked me to pray that they would be given custody of their children or that they would have a healthy baby. Working with these women was one of the most rewarding things I've ever done. But it was also a struggle.

The Bible study was scheduled for 5 p.m. on Thursdays. My boss had given me permission to leave early, but it was nearly impossible to leave the office on time. Then, although the management of the rehab center wanted me there, their wishes didn't filter down to the workers on the women's floor. I usually had trouble getting into the building. Our meeting room was often occupied because the Bible study had somehow been left off the schedule, and I would have to go from room to room and let the women know it was time for our study. It was like pulling teeth to make the meeting happen. Satan would whisper to me, "You are a white, middle-class woman from the suburbs. How do you think you can help these women? What do you know of their problems? And the neighborhood is not safe. You are being foolish." I had to force myself to follow through, but my life was so much richer because I did.

While I was obedient to what I felt God wanted me to do in that particular situation, I have sometimes resisted God's call. I've held back when I knew I should *move*. I've given up on a plan because it didn't come easily. I've chosen not to take time for relationships because it's just too much work. I've chosen to stay in my comfort zone.

If you want to guard against complacency, make a commitment to *do something for others!* Give a check each month to the poor. Sponsor a child or support a homeless shelter or give to a food pantry through your church. Even better, volunteer your time to work at one of those shelters. Nothing makes you appreciate your blessings more than to see up close those less fortunate than yourself. Invite a single mom and her children or someone who could never reciprocate into your home.

One of the greatest joys Jerry and I had as a newly-married couple was to invite recovering alcoholics from a rehab center into our home for Sunday dinner. Most of them had long since destroyed all family relationships and were truly alone. Our home environment was a huge blessing to these men who knew only the cold surroundings of an institution. We spent many pleasant Sunday afternoons with these men who could never return the favor.

We *are* our brother's (and sister's) keeper. When we stand before God, I believe we may be reminded of our lost opportunities to love and bless others. And it won't help to say, "I just didn't think about it." That is the essence of complacency.

Take Good Care of Yourself

You can resist the temptation to complacency regarding your appearance and health by getting into a regular routine of self-care. I know how hard this can be for a young mother with small children, or for a working mother with older children. All of us fight the tyranny of the urgent, but we can't leave taking care of ourselves on the back burner. So determine to keep your weight under control, exercise, get enough sleep, schedule regular health exams, and take some time to rejuvenate.

While true beauty comes from the inside and God looks on the heart, those around us see the outside. There is much we can do to maintain and enhance the way we look. Well-fitted, stylish clothes, cleanliness, a good hairstyle, and appropriate makeup are not optional in my opinion. They are not only essential, but in our society, totally doable—even on the most meager income.

We cannot be salt and light to an ungodly world if our appearance is a distraction. And remember that you should not compare *your best* with someone else's. Simply improve what you can about your appearance and be content with the rest. As you will see later in this chapter, God can use beauty, both inward and outward, for His glory as surely as He can use any other quality.

Try Something New and Scary

One way to fight complacency is to do at least one thing per month that makes you feel uncomfortable. This looks different for each woman. For one it could be approaching a stranger and introducing herself. For another it could be calling a new acquaintance and setting up a lunch date. You might decide to take a class or learn a new skill. It could be losing weight, joining a gym, or getting a makeover.

Whatever you decide to *do* is never as easy as *doing nothing*. But you'll reap the benefits of increased self-esteem and the confidence to step out in obedience to the Lord's direction.

Let us examine the life of one woman who stepped out in obedience but, in so doing, put her own life in jeopardy. May God give us the courage of this little peasant orphan who became queen.

BECOMING A WOMAN OF COURAGE AND DESTINY

Perhaps the most beloved of all the women in the Bible is Queen Esther. She had been brought to the palace of the powerful king of Persia. Esther competed in the most famous beauty contest in history. The girls were preparing themselves to be chosen by the king to replace Vashti, the queen who had fallen into disfavor. Vashti had done the unthinkable. She had refused to obey the king's order to come and be a spectacle for his drunken friends. So Vashti was dismissed and Esther was chosen.

Esther was not a woman of royal birth who ruled next to the king, as we see in later cultures. She was "queen" of the harem — the reigning favorite wife at the time. Can you imagine being one of many, perhaps hundreds of wives? And once you were chosen, you were basically a prisoner for life.

Esther's exalted status did, however, allow her certain privileges. As "queen consort" she was allowed to wear the royal tiara and was the acknowledged head of the female apartments. The other concubines honored her by actual prostration. She had great wealth of her own, not necessarily by the will of the king, but by Persian law. She now wore the splendid attire and extravagant ornamentation of the queen of Persia.[4]

Lovely little Esther, Hebrew orphan that she was, had come a long way from her cousin Mordecai's humble home. She had become very comfortable and accustomed to the luxury of the women's apartments. Though not an ideal lifestyle, Esther had settled in. Perhaps the isolation, routine, boredom, or indulgence had caused her to become complacent in the house of women.

When the villain Haman enters the picture, threatening to annihilate the entire Hebrew race, Mordecai put on the sackcloth and ashes of mourning. But he didn't waste any time asking for Esther's help. She had been chosen as queen and had come to the palace to stand in the gap for her people. She must go to the king and appeal for their lives.

Esther wasn't so sure. She wasn't ready to leap out of her comfort zone to do something so radical. But she was the Jewish people's only hope. Mordecai tried the tactic of appealing to Esther's sense of purpose and destiny. "Who can say but that God has brought you into the palace for just such a time as this?" (Esther 4:14, TLB).

But Esther didn't bite. No way. She knew the law. You didn't just go marching into the king's chambers anytime you wanted. Unless you were summoned, it could mean your immediate execution.

And queen or not, Esther wasn't so sure anymore about where she stood with Xerxes. He hadn't called for her in over a month.

Then Mordecai got practical. He gave his newly exalted cousin a wake-up call. "Think not that in the king's palace you will escape any more than all the other Jews" (4:13, RSV).

If Esther refused to take the risk, it could have cost her *her* life and many others' lives as well. But Esther *did* rise to the occasion and resisted the temptation to remain complacent. She also resisted the temptations of selfishness, paralyzing fear, and refusing to obey God's call. She not only demonstrated outstanding courage to appeal to the king for her people, she also used cunning, wisdom, and a great sense of timing to make it happen. She was incredibly successful. The Hebrew race was saved and Esther found her way into Jewish history.

Have you ever been handed a once-in-a-lifetime opportunity to do something great, but found yourself too timid or unprepared, or just too comfortable where you were to even try? It's interesting to note the steps Esther went through to accomplish her mission — steps we can emulate to become a woman of courage, passion, and destiny.

1. She overcame her fear.

Esther knew her life was in danger, but she had to face her fear and overcome it. So must we if we are to avoid complacency. I realize this is much easier said than done. The first way to overcome your fear is to identify it. What are you really afraid of? Are you afraid of appearing foolish? Are you afraid of other people's criticism, afraid of failure? Is your pride getting in the way of courage? Giving a name to your fear is a good way to put it in perspective. Prayer and meditating on God's promises can also help to alleviate your fears. Scriptures such as this one in Hebrews 13:5-6 are great faith builders:

God has said, "I will never, *never* fail you nor forsake you." That is why we can say without any doubt or fear, "The Lord is my Helper, and I am not afraid of anything that mere men can do to me." (TLB).

Also consider memorizing Psalm 34:4; Matthew 10:28; 2 Timothy 1:7; Luke 12:7; and Luke 12:32.

One way I have overcome fear is to go ahead and imagine the worst thing that could happen. Then I symbolically give that situation to God, knowing that nothing is impossible with Him—and knowing He has promised to help me and make all things work together for my good.

You may never be asked to save a whole race of people. But sooner or later God will ask each of us to do something radical, or at least something that shoves us way out of our comfort zone. "Radical" for some may be standing in front of others to speak or teach. "Radical" for another may be traveling to foreign lands and taking life-threatening risks. Or it may be speaking up when remaining silent is the safer choice. It may be deciding not to give up on a failing marriage or to use tough love on a wayward child. True courage means moving forward in obedience—in spite of your fear.

2. *She had a submissive spirit.*

I don't know if Esther was given a choice about entering the beauty contest, but she went willingly. She submitted herself to Mordecai and went along with the year-long preparations, and then later submitted to the role of Xerxes' wife. When her cousin asked her to appeal to the king, she finally agreed.

Submission and obedience don't come naturally for most of us. But no matter how distasteful it is to us, it's biblical.

I urge you to be subject to such men and to every fellow worker and laborer. (1 Corinthians 16:16, RSV).

> Be subject to one another out of reverence for Christ.
> (Ephesians 5:21, RSV)

Ask God to give you a *submissive spirit*. Being submissive doesn't mean you are weak; it means you are willing to put yourself under God and those in authority over you. It means you have a cooperative attitude, a teachable spirit, and the courage to do something you may not want to do.

3. She sought divine guidance and help from others.

Once Esther decided to move ahead with the dangerous plan, she knew she needed help. Perhaps the most important step she took was to seek divine help and support from others. She asked all the Jews to fast and pray for three days, and she did the same.

If we could only grasp the importance of dependency on God. Much of our complacency stems from fear and lack of confidence. We live in a society that prides itself on being independent. Many women have been influenced to view dependency as a weak and ugly trait. But throughout the Bible, God asked the least likely people to carry out the important missions because He knew they would have to depend on Him. Gideon, Moses, and Jesus' mother, Mary, are examples of those who were inadequate, but with God's help they accomplished the impossible.

Esther knew the importance of prayer support. Never hesitate to ask others to pray for you. When God asks you to step into a risky situation, He will equip you and empower you. But He wants you to admit your inadequacy for the task and rely on Him to accomplish it.

4. She was sensitive to God's timing.

When we give in to the temptation of complacency, we often miss God's timing. It's usually a case of dragging our feet and not obeying quickly enough, but sometimes we can get ahead of God. Esther didn't just walk in and blurt out her request. She had a plan and used patience and wisdom in carrying it out. The result was that the villain Haman was exposed and the king granted her request. Esther's story shows us that the secret to moving in God's timetable is earnest prayer, patience, and listening to the wise counsel of others and the still, small voice of the Lord.

God has a special assignment for each of us. You may be in the midst of high drama, poised on the brink of a mission of enormous magnitude and not even realize it. You may have *come to the kingdom for such a time as this.*

Esther's Steps Toward Significance

- She overcome her fear.
- She was humble and submissive.
- She sought divine guidance and help from others.
- She was sensitive to God's timing.

Friend, I believe you have chosen to read this book on temptation because you desire a life of godliness, passion, and purpose. Don't miss God's best by thinking you can merely coast through life. We are just as susceptible to The Eve Factor when we allow Satan to lull us into inactivity and make us so comfortable we miss our greatest opportunities for ministry and blessing. Get motivated, get moving, be proactive, and soar—right out of your comfort zone and into significance.

CHAPTER FOUR:
OUT OF YOUR COMFORT ZONE
AND INTO SIGNIFICANCE

Study and Explore

Read the story of the Good Samaritan in Luke 10:30-37. Can you think of any modern-day examples of how our complacency plays itself out in a similar way?

Read the following verses, and write down what you learn about complacency and why it is so important to guard against it.

Example: Matthew 24:12 — People will lose their love for God because of sin.

Matthew 24:42
Mark 13:35-37
Luke 21:34

Consider and Reflect

1. Write down at least four words that can describe complacency.

2. What are some of the causes of spiritual complacency?

3. Why do we tend to be more complacent when everything is going well?

4. Do you think God allows trials in our lives to shake us loose from our complacency? Can you think of real life examples?

5. List at least three lies of the Enemy that result in the temptation to give in to complacency. (Example: Staying in a bad situation is better than the risk of change.)

6. Why is it important to develop close friendships? (See Proverbs 27:9; Ecclesiastes 4:9-12; 1 John 3:16; and Proverbs 18:24.)

7. Read the following passages: Matthew 10:27,32-33; Matthew 24:14; Mark 1:8; Mark 16:15; Acts 1:8; Romans 10:15. Why do you think it is important to share our faith with others?

8. Have you succumbed to complacency in some areas? Write a short confession next to the ones that apply to you.

- Marriage
- Friendships
- Reaching out to others
- Health
- Appearance
- Prayer
- Bible study
- Worship
- Fear of trying something new

9. As you look back over your life, make a list of what complacency has cost you.

10. Now that you have been honest about your failures, do the following:

- Confess them to God in prayer.
- Ask God to forgive you.
- Ask for God's help in correcting the failures if possible.
- Forgive yourself.

Pray

Lord Jesus, I have just confessed my complacency and asked for Your forgiveness. I know that You always forgive when I ask with a sincere heart. Now help me to forgive myself. Don't let my failures of the past produce even more fear or complacency. Help me to be more diligent from this day forward to live a life that is pleasing to You and a blessing to those around me. Don't let me miss one single blessing or opportunity You have intended for me because of apathy, laziness, self-righteousness, or fear. Help me to keep our relationship intense, exciting, and active. Help me always be obedient to what You ask me to do, even if it's far out of my comfort zone. In Your name, Amen.

WORRY, GOSSIP, AND THE FEAR FACTOR

The Temptation of Negativity

Whatsoever things are true, . . . whatsoever things are of good report; . . . think on these things.

PHILIPPIANS 4:8, KJV

Several years ago I interviewed a doctor who used a term I had never heard before — *awfulize*. He explained he had made up the word to describe the behavior of many of his patients. If they discover a mole, they are sure it's melanoma. If they have any slight pain, they're convinced they are having a heart attack or have some other serious disease. *To awfulize* is to make things much worse than they actually are.

Awfulizing, which can take the form of fear, worry, or anxiety, is a huge temptation for many women. We awfulize about everything. After all, isn't worrying part of a mother's job description? We pray about our needs, but we don't really expect answers and instead live in dread that what we fear will come true.

All of us are tempted to be negative occasionally. But if you habitually approach life from the dark side and allow worry and fear to control your life, your temptation has become sin. When your cynicism overpowers your faith, you have yielded to temptation and you need forgiveness and deliverance.

Let me give a disclaimer here. I am neither a doctor nor a professional counselor, and I'm not qualified to address conditions such as severe anxiety disorder. Likewise, this chapter will not deal with clinical depression, which the National Mental Health Association cites as affecting more than 19 million American adults each year. My use of "negativity" does not refer to grief—a natural time of sadness or depression following a death or other trauma.

So this discussion is strictly limited to our propensity toward fear, worry, negativity, criticism, and gossip—negative tendencies brought on by Satan, a lack of faith, bad habits, or a naturally pessimistic nature. With that said, let's look at the various ways women give in to the temptation of negativity. As you read, ask the Holy Spirit to show you where you may be vulnerable to this temptation and if you have already succumbed.

How Are We Tempted by Negativity?

A Critical Spirit

Have you ever been around women who seem to criticize everything and everyone? They aren't happy with their pastor or their boss. Their children aren't doing well enough in school, and their friends don't call them enough. Their neighbors don't mow their lawn enough, and their husband isn't spiritual enough.

While constructive criticism is helpful and necessary, the *habit* of debilitating criticism is destructive. While dissatisfaction makes *us* unhappy, a critical spirit makes those around us miserable as well. A critical attitude is always hurtful and alienates others. When the recipient of our excessive criticism is our child, the destruction we cause is profound and debilitating. And when the person we are constantly finding fault with is our husband, it can result in divorce or a miserable marriage. Just ask Chuck.

Mindy and Chuck have been married for over twenty years. He is a man's man who enjoys fishing, hunting, and outdoor activities. He has been very successful in business, but is a little rough around the edges. Mindy is a devoted mother and active in her church. While he's a good man who loves the Lord, Chuck is quiet by nature and isn't involved in any up-front leadership at church.

One day Chuck confided to Jerry and me that Mindy had become so unhappy and so critical of him, he wasn't sure she would stay in the marriage. He was baffled as to how he could make her happy. He said she found fault with everything he did and *didn't* do: He wasn't sensitive enough and he wasn't spiritual enough—she wanted him to be more of a leader in the church.

Chuck admitted he certainly wasn't perfect, but he also said he was honestly trying to be the husband Mindy wanted him to be. He had even committed to going to counseling with his pastor every morning for six weeks to try and grow spiritually and become a better husband. But Mindy was obsessed with the negatives and had fallen into a spirit of criticism. She had unrealistic expectations and had succumbed to dissatisfaction. The resulting negativity bankrupted their relationship. While their marriage did not end, Chuck is frustrated and deeply hurt that his best is still not good enough, and Mindy continues to be unhappy.

Excessive criticism never produces positive results, nor does gossip.

Gossip

Most women have succumbed to the temptation to gossip at one time or another. I know I've been guilty. When we hear a juicy piece of gossip, our first impulse is to tell someone else. Why are we not as driven to spread *good* news? The positives we easily forget—the gossip we remember for years.

One reason we find gossip so tempting is that we think we are building up ourselves by diminishing others. In a twisted way our fleshly nature takes pleasure in criticism and fault-finding, because we can then feel superior. And if we can join together with one or more women who are doing the same thing, it validates us even more. I think we also succumb to this temptation because of our need to connect with other women and share confidences. Gossip gives us something to talk about and a reason to connect, but at someone else's expense.

While most of us would agree that it's wrong to spread lies about other people, we're not so sure if it's wrong to share truthful information about someone for a legitimate purpose. But it *is* wrong, and this story illustrates one reason why.

My friend Nicki told me how "innocently sharing information" got her into big trouble. Her husband, Ken, worked for a couple who had their own business. It was small and struggling, but they treated Ken well. The two couples became friends. However, the employers were always promising growth for the company and bigger things for the future. The growth never happened and Ken eventually moved on to a better job.

One day Nicki ran into an old friend whose husband had just taken a job with Ken's former employers. Nicki felt a need to warn her friend about their experience, and said, "Just be cautious about expecting big things to happen with the company. They never do."

Weeks later, the wife of Ken's old boss called and confronted Nicki. She had learned what Nicki had said and was furious and hurt. She said, "How could you do that to us when we were so good to you and Ken?"

Needless to say, Nicki was mortified and didn't know what to say except, "I'm sorry."

There are times when our words are not necessarily malicious, but they are careless and hurtful nonetheless. We must search our hearts to discover why we need to tell what we know. Was Nicki really trying to help her friends, or was she unconsciously punishing the former employer because she and Ken didn't receive the payoff they had expected? I'm not sure, but I do know this: When we are tempted to give a bad report, we need to be very careful about our motives.

The temptation to gossip is a test of our character. Do we have the discipline to keep our mouths closed and our hearts open to love, forgive, and think the best of others?

Paralyzing Fear

"You have colon cancer." The doctor dropped the bomb on my husband by telephone. I knew by the look on Jerry's face it was bad news.

That day I came face-to-face with my greatest fear. My mother and father had both had cancer and so had Jerry's mother. My secret fear was that someone in our immediate family would get cancer. But what I remember most about the moments following the doctor's call was the tangible presence of the Lord. It was as though He were standing right beside me. I could almost feel a comforting arm around my shoulder—a poignant and reassuring sensation that helped me deal with this devastating news.

However, the first emotion I experienced was fear. It's a natural human emotion, just like anger or happiness. In the last chapter we talked about the fear of taking risks. But fear, when it's akin to terror, tends to paralyze and debilitate. When we give in to that kind of fear, we have given control of our lives over to the Enemy and have succumbed to sin.

By God's grace I did not give in to paralyzing fear. With His help I pushed my fear aside and moved forward in faith. The next weeks were not easy, but they were filled with God's blessings. The strength of the Lord and the prayers of friends and family carried us through the weeks ahead. The colon cancer was a stage B and after a difficult surgery, the doctor told Jerry he would not receive any further treatment, although he faced a fifty-fifty chance of a recurrence. Yet, I had real peace in the midst of those challenging days.

Three months later when Jerry went back for a check-up, the tests revealed more cancer. The doctor saw a shadow over Jerry's liver and suspected that the cancer had spread there. He said if this were true, it wouldn't help to operate. We wouldn't know for eight days.

This time, I hit a wall. I faced a huge test — one that took every ounce of spiritual maturity and tenacity I could muster. The first two days after getting the news that Jerry's cancer could well be terminal, I was devastated — filled with anxiety, depressed, and distracted. My peace had fled like a fair-weather friend. A parade of worst-case scenarios marched continuously through my mind. *Jerry is going to die. You will not be able to support yourself and your children. The kids will never be able to go to college.* And on they came, one worse than the other.

Finally, about the third day, the Holy Spirit got my attention. I came to see my fear for what it was: A temptation directly from Satan — intended to rob me of peace and faith. Satan likes to kick us when we're down. He'll trick us into thinking things are worse than they are. He is the greatest awfulizer of all. He *never* tells the truth. He will try to paralyze us with fear in order to sap every ounce of faith from our soul. He will zero in on the thing that scares us the most.

And then I learned an important lesson: The Word of God can be a powerful weapon to help us resist temptation. I began to renounce those negative thoughts and went to the Bible for strength and comfort. God gave me two Scriptures I clung to that very long week.

Finally, brothers, whatever is true, whatever noble, whatever is right, whatever is pure, whatever is lovely, whatever is admirable—if anything is excellent or praiseworthy—think about such things. (Philippians 4:8)

When you pass through the waters I will be with you; and through the rivers, they shall not overwhelm you; when you walk through fire you shall not be burned, and the flame shall not consume you. For I am the LORD your God, the Holy one of Israel, your Savior. (Isaiah 43:2-3, RSV)

When Satan brought a negative thought, I would say, "Yes, we're walking through the fire, but God promised we wouldn't be burned. We are in deep waters now, but we will not drown." I clung to the truth that whatever happened, I and our children would be okay. God would give us what we needed.

I passed this challenging test of faith, but it took all my spiritual resources. I was doing battle, fighting for my very life, emotionally and spiritually. I refused to accept the fear, because I know fear is never from God.

Spiritual warfare is not something spooky that requires special training or some weird ritual. James 4:7 says if we resist the Devil, he will flee from us. Beth Moore gets to the core of the issue:

In any warfare waged by the enemy against the individual believer, the primary battlefield is the *mind*. . . . The enemy's chief target is the mind because the most effective way to influence behavior is to influence thinking.[1]

The spoken Word of God is a powerful weapon against the temptations of the Enemy. Did I sail happily through the rest of the week? No. I was still concerned. I was anxious to see what the test results would be. But I slept soundly. I was able to offer genuine encouragement and support to Jerry, who was fighting his own battle with the Enemy. And I could go about my daily tasks normally, walking in faith and expecting God to provide whatever my family needed in the days ahead. Satan lost that round.

When we went back to the doctor, he told us the shadow on Jerry's liver was merely a piece of colon lying across it. Jerry had a second surgery to remove the additional malignancy, and fifteen years later he is still blessed with good health.

I realize our cancer story might have had a very different ending. Christians *do* die of cancer, other illnesses, or accidents, and perhaps you are in the midst of your grief over that kind of loss. Still, I believe if God had chosen to take Jerry to heaven instead of healing his body, the Holy Spirit would have been my comforter and God would have provided for us.

While fear can be debilitating, it usually has a face and a name and eventual closure. Worry can be more troublesome because it can be more open-ended and may not be tied to anything specific.

Worry

From the age of twelve our son had an unusual, God-given interest in the Middle East and the Jewish people. Jeff even studied Hebrew on his own and with a tutor. After college he got a job right away, but his dad and I sensed he was unhappy. He said more than anything he wanted to live in Israel for a time so he could become fluent in Hebrew.

With our encouragement, Jeff went to Israel and lived on a kibbutz. He worked in the olive groves, in the kitchen, and other areas. He had a tiny dorm room with sparse furnishings and a concrete floor, and he made no money except a small stipend. But he was blissfully happy because he was in the land he loved, doing what he had always wanted. After about four months, to our surprise, Jeff was accepted at Yavneh, a center for Jewish studies. It was an ultra-orthodox environment where everyone was Jewish and had to follow very strict rules. But he enjoyed it immensely.

However, for a couple of months between the assignments, Jeff lived alone in Safed, doing odd jobs for his rent, barely managing to make ends meet. Even though he was in his twenties, I sometimes worried about him. Did he have enough money? There were many anxious moments like the time the ATM machine ate his card and another time when we wired him money that was delivered to the wrong town. Did he have enough food? Would he step on a landmine or encounter a terrorist? But most of the time I resisted worrying about Jeff and put him in God's hands.

After a year Jeff returned home, fluent in Hebrew, to pursue his master's degree. We were happy to have our son home, but were in for quite a shock. He was wearing a yamekah and a talith (prayer shawl) and praying his Hebrew prayers. He informed us he was converting to Judaism!

Talk about a plan backfiring! What had I done, giving my blessing on this Israel adventure—just to have my son reject Jesus and embrace the religion of the Old Testament! While our family has always had a deep appreciation and love for the Jews and Judaism and have traveled many times to the Holy Land, we are deeply committed to our evangelical beliefs.

I could not believe this was happening. I became distraught, and knew I was yielding to negativity. But then Jerry and I decided that instead of trying to preach to Jeff, we would continue to trust God for our son. Instead of fretting, we would pray earnestly for him. Oh, we always prayed for our children..But we began serious intercession, doing spiritual battle for Jeff every day. As I prayed for our son, I gradually got hold of a true sense of peace. I knew he had a deep love for God and that his search was a sincere one. I felt sure God would lead him to the truth.

Then one day we got our miracle. Jeff called home from the seminary he was attending to say he could not convert to Judaism. He had found the Messiah in the Old and New Testaments and he knew He was Jesus.

As a parent of three adult children and six grandchildren, I can assure you the temptation to worry about your offspring never goes away. They remain our Achilles' heel forever. We worry our kids will marry the wrong person. We are afraid they will choose the wrong career or not be able to find a job. We worry when they leave home and we worry they will *never* leave. We worry about their grades, their friends, their health, and we *really* worry when they get behind the wheel! Perhaps our greatest worry is when they stray from their faith and fail to embrace our morals and value system—and most do, at least for short periods of time. After all, we live in a world filled with real threats from terrorists, war, a fragile economy, drugs, promiscuity, sexually transmitted diseases, and ungodliness. But when worry becomes habitual instead of occasional, it can affect our health and certainly impacts our effectiveness as Christians.

I recently found an interesting definition of the verb *worry* in my dictionary: "To seize with the teeth and shake or pull about as in *the dog was worrying a rat.*"[2] I had not heard *worry* used in that context since my childhood in the Deep South. But how appropriate it is! That's exactly what Satan does with our minds and emotions when he tempts us to worry. He grabs us with his teeth and jerks us around, harassing us, and toying with us just for the fun of it.

Don't let the bondage of worry ruin your life and your peace. It's a temptation you *can* resist. The next time you are tempted to worry, remember that even when we can't see a solution, God has one.

Doubt

Kayanne Janiga is a nurse and experienced family therapist. She has observed in her practice that one of the most serious side effects of negativity is that women often transfer their doubt, uncertainty, and lack of faith and hope to the Lord. They are never quite sure if God is faithful or if He'll be there in thick and thin, or that He can really be trusted.[3]

Does your pessimism override your faith and trust? Do you believe the voice of the Enemy more than you believe God's Word? Are your prayers being answered? Time after time in Scripture when someone desired to receive something from Jesus, it was his or her *faith* that brought the answer (Matthew 9:22; Matthew 15:28; Mark 10:52; Luke 5:20). James makes it clear we should believe when we pray:

> But when he asks, he must believe and not doubt, because he who doubts is like a wave of the sea, blown and tossed by the wind. That man should not think he will receive anything from the Lord. (1:6-7)

How can you know whether you've let doubt and pessimism interfere with your relationship with God? By looking honestly at the attitude of your heart. Have you succumbed to The Eve Factor and doubted God's Word? Do you really believe that all things work together for good? (See Romans 8:28.) Do you *live* it? Matthew 7:20 (KJV) says, "By their fruits ye shall know them." What is the fruit of your life? Are you leaving a legacy of joy and confidence to your children, or is your example one of criticism and defeat? Are you at peace most of the time, or are worry and depression your constant companions? Are you an encourager or do you drag others down? Galatians 5:22 says, "The fruit of the spirit is love, joy, peace." If that's not what your fruit looks like, you've yielded to temptation and let your negativity interfere with your faith.

I don't know of any woman who likes worrying or being gripped by fear and negativity, so why is this such a problem for us? Why do we allow ourselves to fall into negative thinking when it brings such unhappiness? I think several factors make us susceptible to this temptation.

What Makes Us Susceptible?

Again, a poor self-image makes us vulnerable to many temptations. Self-doubt and a lack of confidence cloud our perspective on everything. But our temperament can also increase our vulnerability to the temptation of negativity.

The personality type most vulnerable is the Melancholy. Their very nature is pessimistic, and they tend to think the worst. But optimistic Sanguines can easily fall into gossip and a critical spirit because we just can't resist a good story, Phlegmatics can lean toward cynicism, and Cholerics often fret about not accomplishing enough.

However, there is another source of negativity you may not have considered. I was curious why this problem seemed so widespread, even among Christian women. I asked Mrs. Janiga if this was, in fact, a common problem and why. Her answer surprised me. She said the tendency toward negativity, anxiety, and even panic disorder is often a case of learned behavior passed on by mothers and grandmothers. She said, "When we grow up in the atmosphere of negativity and anxiety, we learn these scripts well and begin approaching our own life experiences with insecurity and uncertainty."[4]

We mothers must be careful about our attitude and the way we approach life. Are we teaching our children, particularly our daughters, to be afraid, to worry, and to imagine the worst-case scenario? Or are we projecting confidence, optimism, and strong faith in God? We can leave them a legacy of happiness and confidence or one of fear and anxiety. Ask yourself if *your* negativity is a pattern you learned from *your* mother and if you are perpetuating it. In addition, build some safeguards that can help you resist this temptation when it comes knocking on your door.

Building Safeguards Against Negativity

Here are some ways you can bolster your resistance to this temptation and build safeguards to prevent it.

Bring Your Thoughts into Captivity

The key to a positive, optimistic outlook and victory over negativity lies in not accepting the negative thoughts in the first place. This takes determination, strong resolve, and *practice!* Especially when you have succumbed to paralyzing fear. But it *can* be done. Resist the devil and see how quickly he flees (see James 4:7). Each time we resist him, it gets a little easier. Don't let him play games with your mind. Ask God to make your spiritual antennae so sensitive that when worry or fear creeps in, you immediately recognize it and resist it before it can immobilize you and destroy your faith. Paul says we can "take captive every thought to make it obedient to Christ" (2 Corinthians 10:5). When we let paralyzing fear control our lives, we are not being obedient to Christ.

Don't Say Anything if You Can't Say Something Good

This is a good safeguard for keeping our criticism and gossip under control. Don't speak words that can be potentially damaging to someone; instead pray for that person. If there is someone you just don't like, who rubs you the wrong way, pray for her. I know it's not easy, but put forth the effort and God will help you. I've tried it; it works! Pretty soon the critical thoughts will diminish and your prayers for her will become heartfelt and fervent.

Don't fall into the trap of seeing only the faults of others and succumb to a critical spirit. Rejoice in and focus on the strengths of your husband, your children, your friends, neighbors, coworkers, *and yourself*. If you are prone to a critical spirit, develop the habit of praise and appreciation. Look for the good in others, and if you can't say something good, don't say anything at all.

Just as important, don't believe the negative comments directed toward you by others. Refuse to let negativity injure your spirit or confidence. We must guard our hearts against hurtful words, and filter the criticism we receive through our knowledge of God's love for us and of our priceless value to Him. If someone hurts your feelings, don't let the damaging words get into your spirit and fester. We can't help being hurt, but we can, with God's help, release the hurt quickly and move on.

God's Word says:

Be devoted to one another in brotherly love. Honor one another above yourselves. (Roman 12:10)

My command is this: Love each other as I have loved you. (John 15:12)

If you feel you have a critical spirit, read 1 Corinthians 13 (the love chapter) every single day. Memorize these verses, repent of your criticism, and pray for a double portion of Christ's love for others.

Give Your Worry to God

You may think living free of worry in today's troubled world is impossible, but Jesus Himself gave us a wonderful example of "peace in the midst of a storm." When He told His disciples farewell the night before His crucifixion, he said, "Do not let your hearts be troubled. Trust in God; trust also in me" (John 14:1). He knew full well what He and the disciples faced in the days ahead, yet He told them not to be troubled. He gave His dear friends—and us—final words of advice and encouragement.

He went on to tell them that He was also leaving them a legacy of joy, love, and peace. "I am leaving you with a gift—peace of mind and heart! And the peace I give isn't fragile like the peace the world gives. So don't be troubled or afraid" (14:27, TLB). *The Simple English* translation reads, "I am giving you my peace." Jesus faced the cross—the most horrific, torturous death ever devised. As God, Jesus knew His death would mean Satan's ultimate defeat. He knew this was why He came to earth, and that He would soon return to His Father in heaven. But as a man, He saw the agony ahead and dreaded it. Later that night He asked God to try to find another way (Matthew 26:39). Yet Jesus had peace. And He promised to give His peace to us.

Trust God with Your Children

Worrying about your children does nothing but add gray to your hair and wrinkles to your forehead. But battling in prayer for them makes a huge difference. Worrying is passive; praying is active. Philippians 4:6 says not to worry about anything, but to pray about everything. And then give thanks for the answer. This simple command is at the heart of *joyful* parenting.

Worry is the opposite of trust. We either trust our children to God, or we worry and fret our way through life. Oswald Chambers makes this interesting observation about worry: "Fretting springs from a determination to get our own way."[5] Ouch! Could much of our fretting over our children stem from a desire to get our own way? Granted, *our* way would be for only *good* things to happen. But what if our idea of the best is not God's? It's difficult to see our children go through pain, but most of us who have many years of mothering under our belts have learned God can use adversity to accomplish His ultimate plan in the lives of our kids.

I realize this sounds idealistic if you have a child who is in deep trouble and hurting. I know because I've been there. If you have a child who is seriously ill, or a teen on drugs, or a runaway, or a son or daughter living in an abusive marriage, you need help and support NOW! Sometimes you are in such a panic you cannot even pray. Depend on your pastor and Christian friends to hold you up. "Let him have all your worries and cares, for he is always thinking about you and watching everything that concerns you" (1 Peter 5:7, TLB). Isn't that a comforting thought? The Lord is always thinking about us and He understands. He cares about our children and grandchildren. We can trust their future to Him.

Pray with Faith and Never Give Up

Do you really believe God hears your prayers? Or is prayer just a habit, or an extension of your uncertainty, a little added insurance for your hopes and wishes? Faith and doubt cannot coexist. Doubt cancels out faith.

Answers to our prayers don't always come right away. God certainly doesn't work according to our timetable. Oswald Chambers insightfully wrote: "If God, who is perfect, can be patient with me even though I am imperfect, why can't I be patient with Him?"[6]

Yet, many times we aren't patient. We pray for the salvation of our loved ones, only to give up as the years go by. Or we make some attempts to be obedient to a call of God on our life, but it never works out and we begin to think it never will.

God's Word has something to say to you if you have been sowing years of prayer and not received a harvest yet. "Let us not be weary in well doing: for in due season we shall reap, if we faint not" (Galatians 6:9, KJV). We *shall* reap if we don't lose faith. But Satan slips in the negativity and our doubts crowd out our faith.

At the age of eight I came to know the Lord at a small, neighborhood church as a result of an invitation from a neighbor. When my spiritual journey began I immediately started praying for my parents to begin theirs. But it didn't happen for many years.

As an elderly man, my father got Alzheimer's. But in the early days after his diagnosis, when he was lucid most days, he prayed to receive Christ. It was not the salvation experience I would have chosen, but I am confident my dad is in heaven today. God did answer my prayer for him.

A short while after my father passed away, my mother surprised us all by expressing an interest in joining us on our next Israel tour. We certainly understood her wanting to do a little traveling after caring for my father for seven years. But the Holy Land? My mother had mellowed over the years since my childhood conversion, but still did not know the Lord. She had not been to church in many years and never even spoke of spiritual matters.

When I told Jerry my mom wanted to go to Israel with us, he declared, "Your mom is going to accept Christ and I'm going to baptize her in the Jordan River!" What a prophet! That is exactly what happened. Along with about a dozen others on our tour, my mother prayed, asking the Lord to forgive her sins and be her Lord and Savior. On her birthday, at seventy-two years of age, my mom was baptized in the Jordan River in Israel, wearing a rented white robe, her hotel shower cap, and a grin from ear to ear! She couldn't have looked more beautiful.

My mother changed instantly. We developed a closeness we had never had. A few years later, when she learned she had cancer, she exhibited amazing faith and courage. The last words she uttered on this earth were a prayer.

God answered my prayers for my mom and dad's salvation, but it took over forty years! Never, never give up. Especially in praying for those you love to come to faith in Christ. Satan will tell you it will never happen. He will bring discouragement, unbelief, and despair. He will tell you God is not real, your faith is meaningless, and your prayers are a waste of time. Don't listen.

Instead, become a woman of peace and joy who places complete trust in God.

BECOMING A WOMAN OF PEACE, JOY, AND TRUST

The most well-known mother in history—Mary, the mother of Jesus—provides us with the best example of ultimate trust in God. When the angel Gabriel appeared to her, telling her she would become pregnant, she may have been just a young teenager. Yet she knew God and trusted Him with her future. On learning about the pregnancy, Mary asked only one question, "But how can I have a baby? I am a virgin" (Luke 1:34, TLB). Just a simple little biological question. Understandable. And I don't think the angel gave her a very good answer.

"The angel answered, 'The Holy Spirit shall come upon you, and the power of God shall overshadow you'" (verse 35). I think I might have said, "Is there someone else I can talk to?" But Mary seemed to accept the answer, even though she didn't fully understand. We are given no indication that she was worried about what her family, friends, or even Joseph would think. In fact, when Mary arrived at her cousin Elizabeth's home, she proclaimed her glorious acceptance and *joy*: "Oh, how I praise the Lord. How I rejoice in God my Savior!" (Luke 1:46-47). She accepted her calling and was at peace. That is quite remarkable, given the times and culture she lived in.

What were Mary's qualities that caused God to choose her above all the other women on earth? Though a simple, peasant girl, she had an amazingly positive attitude and virtues worth imitating.

She knew God's Word and lived close to Him. She embraced the promises of God. Could it be we let worry and fear creep in because we don't know God's Word? Scriptures like this one in Jeremiah should give us hope and an optimistic attitude. "For I know the plans I have for you says the Lord. They are plans for good and not for evil, to give you a future and a hope." (Jeremiah 29:11, TLB).

She trusted God. Mary could have been stoned at the city gate for being pregnant and unmarried. But she accepted the angel's message with peace and confidence. She trusted God with her future.

She submitted herself to God's will. Mary's life took a radical turn from what she expected. She humbly accepted God's plan though she didn't understand. When our life gets out of our control, we get upset, depressed, and may even turn our back on God. Some of our negativity may be because we demand our own way and don't want to accept God's will.

She chose joy. Mary could have been worried or anxious. But she saw the blessings in the direction her life had taken. Yes, there was pain, but it did not negate the profound role she played in human history. She chose to enjoy the journey.

Mary's Secrets to Peace and Joy

- She had a relationship with God and knew His Word.
- She trusted God with her future.
- She submitted to God's will for her life.
- She chose joy.

I want to end this chapter with a reality check. I know firsthand that life can get very difficult, yet this book has been written from a Sanguine's perspective. Perhaps you are in such pain that at this moment you are in survival mode and powerless to shake the dark cloud that engulfs you. Take heart. The dark clouds will dissipate if you continue to seek the Lord with all your heart. God loves you just as you are, and He understands.

Oswald Chambers said:

One of the most shallow petty things that can be said is, "every cloud has a silver lining." There are some clouds that are black all through. At the wall of the world stands God with his arms outstretched; and when a man or woman is driven there, the consolations of Jesus Christ are given.[7]

Whatever you may be going through, embrace the consolations of Jesus. He can carry you until you are able to get beyond your despair. You may be in pain, but only for a season. God never wastes pain, and the end of the story is life and victory. Trust Him.

Do these simple principles guarantee we will never have a day of worry or sadness in our lives? Of course not. We're human. We all experience concern, disappointment, illness, and tragedy. As long as we are on this earth we will have to deal with the bad stuff. But when we recognize and overcome the temptation of negativity, we can enjoy God's blessings freely. Joy and peace become the norm, not the exception. We become encouragers—not hindrances to those around us. And we can face challenges with supernatural courage and peace. We can emerge from the dark tunnels of life with our faith and confidence intact, a prayer of thanksgiving on our lips, and a genuine smile on our faces.

CHAPTER FIVE:
WORRY, GOSSIP, AND THE FEAR FACTOR

Study and Explore

Read the following promises for insight into why Christians should have a positive outlook. These are only a few of hundreds in the Bible.

Job 8:21
Psalm 37:24
Psalm 46:1-3
Psalm 55:22
Proverbs 3:25-26
Jeremiah 29:11
Nahum 1:7
John 16:33
Romans 8:37-39
Hebrews 13:6

Look up the following and write down what each has to say about worry and faith:

Matthew 9:22
Matthew 15:28
Mark 10:52
Luke 5:20
John 14:1,27
James 1:6-7
Philippians 4:6-8
1 Peter 5:7

Consider and Reflect

1. Write out your own definition of worry.

2. What is the difference between fear and worry?

3. Read Romans 12:2 and 2 Corinthians 10:5. How can we become more positive by taking control of our thought patterns?

4. How can reading and meditating on the Bible help us overcome fear and worry?

5. Why do you think we tend to focus on others' faults instead of their strengths?

6. Do you criticize your children or your husband more often than you praise them? Make a list of positive traits in each of your children and in your husband, and commit to communicating those qualities to each of them regularly.

7. How can we neutralize the damaging effects of necessary criticism of our children?

8. Do you consider yourself primarily a positive or negative person?

9. Put a check by the ways your negativity has manifested itself.

   - Fear
   - Anxiety

- Worry
- Criticism
- Gossip
- Awfulizing

10. Can you remember a time when worry or fear affected your ability to fulfill your day-to-day activities? How long did that last? How did you deal with it? Did the thing that worried you actually come to pass?

11. Make a list of all the things about which you are worried or afraid, both large and small. This can include finances, unsaved loved ones, children, health, or anything. If there is something niggling at your peace that you can't quite identify, ask the Lord to bring it to mind so you can add it to the list. Then take each one to the Lord in prayer. The next time a negative thought comes, thank God for the answer and resist the Enemy's lies. Think of a positive outcome and give thanks (Philippians 4:8).

Pray

Lord, I confess I often fall prey to the snare of negativity. Forgive my lack of trust and faith in You. Forgive me for unnecessary criticism, fault-finding, and gossip. Help me to focus on the strengths of my husband, children, and others around me. Help me to guard my speech from destructive, worst-case scenarios. Let others know me for my positive, hopeful words of encouragement. Break the cycle of negativity in my life and help me to accept the joy and peace You've promised. In Your name, Amen.

CHAPTER SIX

MORALS, MONEY, MINISKIRTS, AND MIRACLES

The Temptation of Conformity

*Do not conform any longer to the pattern of this world, but be
transformed by the renewing of your mind. Then you will be able to test
and approve what God's will is—his good, pleasing and perfect will.*

ROMANS 12:2

When I was a teenager I read a book that impacted my
life—Charles Sheldon's *In His Steps*. This book gave
me, and thousands of others, the inspiration to
approach every situation with this question, "What would Jesus
do?" I learned a lot about my spiritual commitment, and as a young
Christian I began to make better spiritual decisions.

I was delighted when a few years ago we began to see a resurgence
of that poignant message—what would Jesus do? WWJD bracelets and
bumper stickers are popular today. But is the average Christian woman
living her life like Jesus would? If a spiritual seeker looks to us for a
reason to follow Christ, can she distinguish those who call themselves
Christians from those who don't? Do we look and act differently, or have
we camouflaged our faith because that's easier than taking a stand?

The British scholar and Bible expositor John Stott once said, "Perhaps the greatest hindrance to world evangelism remains our failure to be what we profess to be." It's sobering to see the growing number of women who are giving in to the temptation to compromise their standards and conform to the world.

When it comes to our values, what we allow in our homes, how we spend our money, or even how we dress, many Christian women think and act just like everyone else. We watch the same television shows and movies — the networks say the people in the Bible belt watch the same shows as those in New York and Boston. We read the same smutty novels and magazines. We get the same number of divorces. We have abandoned Christ's command to be in the world but not of it (John 17:15-16) one small compromise at a time. Here's a case in point.

Margaret was a beautiful woman with two adorable children. She loved her husband; he was a great father, but he traveled a lot with his job. In fact, he sometimes had to spend weeks at a time in another country. Margaret considered herself a Christian and worked with a women's group in her church. However, she began feeling sorry for herself because her husband wasn't around all the time.

During this time she started watching daytime soap operas. Her own beauty had always been important to her — it was the way she measured her self-worth — and she admired the glamorous women on the soaps. She watched how they schemed and manipulated and got everything they wanted.

One day when her husband was out of town, Margaret just happened to think of an old boyfriend. (Who do you suppose put that thought into her head?) She remembered that Gary had always been crazy about her and had made her feel like a queen, and she decided to give him a call. Just a phone call to help ease her loneliness — nothing more.

Gary was thrilled to hear from her and told her he still cared deeply for her. He invited her to come and spend the weekend with him. At first Margaret wrestled with the decision and felt incredibly guilty. But she so wanted to feel special and pampered again. Besides, it served her husband right for never paying any attention to her. What harm could one weekend of fun be?

Having convinced herself that she was justified, Margaret found a sitter and took a plane to be with Gary. He was wealthy and flooded her with attention, buying her jewelry and taking her to the most expensive places. Their on-again-off-again affair lasted seven years. Margaret would run off with Gary for a time and then be so guilt-ridden she would go back to her husband and children. Then Gary would call her and the allure of the forbidden fruit was more than she could resist. Finally her husband couldn't take it anymore. They divorced and he got the children.

And Margaret? She lost everything—including Gary. Oh, he did marry her, but after a couple of months he told her he didn't want to be married anymore. It had only been the thrill of the chase for him.

This Christian wife and mom never set out to have an affair, but she yielded to one "little" temptation at a time. She first said "yes" to negativity and dissatisfaction, then to compromise, then to comparison, and back to compromise. By the time Gary invited her to spend the weekend with him, it didn't seem that big of a leap to say "yes" to a full-blown affair.

Sadly, Margaret's story is not an isolated event. Let's take a closer look at the various ways Christian women fall into this trap.

How Are We Tempted to Compromise?

How do well-meaning women allow little temptations and sins to turn into full-blown compromise? And why do we yield? There are several ways we conform.

Adopt the World's Values

As Christians, our standards should be miles above those of the postmodern society we live in. But according to Barna Research Group, the views of those who call themselves Christians differ little from the world on moral issues such as abortion, homosexuality, divorce, pornography, drunkenness, marital affairs, sexual fantasies, and cohabitation.[1] The differences are greater with "born-again" Christians, but still the statistics are appalling. How can we believe the Bible and be so soft on sin?

Our society prides itself on being tolerant. If Christians take a firm stand and embrace moral absolutes, we are often seen as being narrow and intolerant — even by other believers. I saw an example of this recently when Total Living Network televised a town hall meeting on the topic of same-sex marriage. The audience and panel of guests was a balance of opponents and proponents. After the show a woman in the audience came up to Jerry and said, "I'm a born-again Christian, but I think your position is too harsh. You are too intolerant."

I disagree. When Christians move away from our convictions regarding biblical principals of morality and buy into the world's view on tolerance, we are yielding to the temptation of conformity — and sin is sure to follow.

One of the ways I've seen Christian women yield to the temptation of conformity is by allowing their teens to watch movies or television shows or listen to music they know are not good for them. When my youngest child was in high school, we didn't allow her to watch R-rated movies. I was appalled to discover she was occasionally watching very unacceptable movies at her friends' homes. These friends went to the same Christian school and their parents were Christians. But their standards were lower than what I felt comfortable with. How often do we hear from our teens, "Mom, all my friends have seen that movie. Why can't I? It's not that bad." Or "There's nothing wrong with this outfit. It doesn't show that much skin. You're just being mean and too strict."

So we let our teenage sons dress like rock singer wannabes and our thirteen-year-old daughters dress like twenty-five-year-olds. Even though we feel uncomfortable letting our daughter show so much skin, or get a tattoo, or body piercing, we give in because that's what all the kids are doing these days. So we tell ourselves, "Maybe I *am* being too strict. Sally is such a good student. I don't want to say 'no' to everything. If I give in to this, maybe she won't rebel. At least she's not on drugs." Such rationalizations lead to compromise.

We're afraid to tell our kids "no," even though we've been told a hundred times by experts that our children really *want* us to give them boundaries. That they will push against those boundaries, but too much freedom makes them feel insecure.

When my daughter was a young teen and going through a rebellious time, Vanessa often pushed the envelope with the way she dressed. We had a lot of arguments about her clothes, makeup, and hair. But one day she surprised me by saying, "Mom, just tell me if I ever look like a hooker." (As if I wouldn't.) She wanted to dress as close to the line as she could without crossing over it. Do you allow your daughter to dress immodestly because her friends dress that way? It's easy to conform to what the other mothers allow; it's hard to hold your children to stricter standards.

And what about the way *we* dress? Do we show as much cleavage as the women on television? Do we wear our skirts so short they practically disappear when we sit down? Do we wear clothes that overemphasize certain parts of our body? We can be feminine, pretty, and stylish without crossing over the line of compromise.

I'd also like to point out another way Christian women compromise—one that shocked me. A large number of them are getting abortions. One source cites 225,000 Christian women abort each year. Some of these women get the abortions without telling anyone; others are pressured into it by the baby's father. Still others are ushered through the doors of the abortion clinic by their own mothers who just cannot accept the shattering of their idyllic dreams by an unwanted pregnancy.[2]

Why are so many mothers pushing their daughters toward destroying their own grandchildren? According to the research done by Catherine Hickem, founder of Kingdom Princess Ministries, the number one reason is this:

> Their mothers' belief that having this baby would ruin their daughters' lives. These young, frightened, hurting young women were told two things over and over again: they would never have the life they dreamed of and their mothers would not be around to help raise this child.[3]

These mothers succumb to the lie that if their daughter gets an abortion, they can escape the embarrassment. Their perfect "Christian" façade will not be shattered. They think their daughter will be spared the consequences of her actions. So they compromise their values for convenience and the quick fix of abortion. But God has a better way.

I am a mother who knows firsthand the heartbreak of hearing her teenage daughter say, "Mom, I'm pregnant." As tears rolled down her face, Vanessa handed me a letter, explaining that although she and her boyfriend had wanted to keep their relationship pure, they had made a mistake and she was pregnant. She went on to say she would understand if we never spoke to her again, but that she needed our help and support. When I looked up from the letter, she said, "Mom, we didn't mean for this to happen, but it *has* happened. And if we don't want this baby, she'll know. We cannot reject her."

The news hit me in the chest like a two-by-four. I didn't know if I should cry, scream, hug her, or crumple to the floor in a heap. At the same moment, her boyfriend Greg was telling Jerry the news. Of course, we were both devastated. Vanessa is our only daughter. Her news evoked feelings of anger, disappointment, and shattered dreams.

That evening the four of us sat and talked for several hours, but an abortion was never discussed. None of us even considered it. By the time Greg went home and Vanessa went to bed, we were convinced the kids were repentant. They wanted to put God first and provide a Christian home for their child. They had asked for God's forgiveness and ours. What else could we do but give it and move forward?

We all yield to temptation and fall into sin at times. Some sins are just more visible than others. Who were we to condemn Greg and Vanessa? Jerry and I had a choice. We could choose to stay angry, bitter, or vindictive and try to punish these two teenagers, or we could follow the Lord's example and forgive them. And Vanessa was right. We had to think of the baby. This was our grandchild, an innocent baby who deserved a good start and a normal life.

Still, we didn't want to compromise. We didn't want to sweep their sin under the rug. How could we demonstrate forgiveness and support to our kids without appearing to minimize or excuse their sin? We were faced with dozens of questions. Should we give Vanessa and Greg a church wedding or a quiet private ceremony? Would our pastor be willing to perform the ceremony? If we did decide to have a wedding, how could we pull it off in three weeks? Who should we invite? How should we tell our staff? Our friends? Our families? Would it be a sin for Vanessa to wear a wedding dress? A white dress?

Jerry is not only a minister; he is a highly recognized television personality. At the time he had a staff of about 100. Many people would be watching how we handled this. Would they blame us and think we had been bad parents? Would this news have a negative effect on our future ministry?

Despite our concerns, we trusted in the knowledge that when we do what's right, God will help and show us each step to take. Greg and Vanessa decided to send a letter along with the wedding invitations, stating why the wedding was happening so soon. They asked for forgiveness for disappointing anyone, and asked for their prayers. The wedding itself was bathed in emotion and a sweet sense of God's presence.

The newlyweds were true to their word. They became active in our local church and made every effort to put God in the center of their marriage. They were still teenagers, but they showed a maturity that continually amazed me. I could not have been prouder of them.

We saw God use this pregnancy to turn the hearts of two young people back to Himself. After the wedding Vanessa and Greg lived with us. Though they could not support themselves, they gave generously to the church and to missions. Greg distinguished himself at his company and moved up quickly. One year after the wedding, Greg, Vanessa, and baby Macey moved into their own apartment. A year after that, they purchased a humble, but charming little home of their own.

Vanessa looks back on this time and says, "God took our sin and turned it into blessing." She and Greg believe the reason for their financial blessings was their sacrificial giving to the church and to missions. They had many struggles, but theirs is an amazing story of God's grace and help during the young couple's rapid journey to adulthood.

Take note of this very important postscript. If you have encouraged your daughter to get an abortion, or you have had one yourself, get this sin out into the open. If you have not already done so, ask God to forgive you. When you ask with a sincere heart, *He will forgive*. So give Him your guilt and pain, forgive yourself, and move forward toward healing. I strongly recommend you read *A Time to Speak* by Yvonne Florczak-Seeman. Work your way through this healing journal, and seek professional counseling if necessary. Do whatever it takes to put the pain behind you.

Adopt the World's View of Money and Possessions

A recent guest on my *Aspiring Women* program understands the subtle lure of possessions. Abby is a delightful and beautiful young woman who lives an urban lifestyle in downtown Chicago. A strong Christian who is active with her singles group at church, Abby works for a not-for-profit agency that helps women and children. The organization doesn't pay well, and Abby makes less money than most of her friends. During our interview she talked about being raised in a pastor's home and never having much money growing up. She said she always wanted *things*, and that it was important to her to have nice furniture and accessories. Her low income didn't stop her from eating out two or three times a week and buying a car beyond her means. She bought a lot of clothes and lived in a lovely apartment. In fact, Abby admits she worshiped the idol of beauty.

There was nothing wrong with Abby wanting to possess nice things. The potential sin was in how *much* she wanted them and *why*. As a Sanguine, Abby needed to be accepted and loved by her friends, to be a part of the group. She admits she fell into the temptation of comparison and felt relative deprivation compared to what her friends had.

So, Abby watched her credit card debt climb until she realized she was in real trouble. She finally hired a consultant to help her get a handle on her spending. She was shocked to learn she was spending $400 a month above her income! The other sobering discovery was that she wasn't being generous to others. She worked for a ministry supported by people who gave, yet she wasn't helping others herself.

It has taken her a couple of years of hard work and discipline, but Abby is doing much better today. God is helping her *wait* for the nice things she wants, and she is experiencing the freedom of living within her means. She has learned how good it feels to share with others and is allowing the Lord to fill her deepest desires.

Like Abby, many women are tempted by money and possessions. We live in a culture that tells us possessions pave the way to the good life. If we are not on guard, we can easily succumb to the lie that says if we can decorate our homes perfectly, or dress in beautiful, classy clothes, or join the country club, then we will be happy and valued. But possessions never satisfy, particularly when they result in overspending and debt. What we thought would make us happy only leaves us feeling empty and depressed.

I'm not saying that money is evil. We all know it's a necessary part of life. It's the *love* of money and possessions that's wrong because it encourages us to make choices that not only hurt ourselves, but also our families. As a result, fathers put their career and money before their families. Mothers of small children work outside the home in order to buy more and more. When we worship the god of materialism, we confuse our *needs* with our *wants*. First Timothy 6:9-10 describes the danger well:

> But people who long to be rich soon begin to do all kinds of wrong things to get money, things that hurt them and make them evil-minded and finally send them to hell itself. For the love of money is the first step toward all kinds of sin. (TLB)

It's not just those who are greedy or seek to be rich who can succumb to the temptation to adopt the world's values about money. It's also those who are in financial need. Sometimes when money is short, we tend to be more obsessed with it than when we are financially stable. We let worry rob us of peace, make us difficult to live with, and hurt us spiritually. A woman's faith shines the brightest when she can be content in the lean times. The Bible says God will supply *all* our needs. We must learn to live within our means and trust God to provide for us.

Adopt the World's Standard of Beauty

Several years ago I interviewed Patrika Darbo, an actress and former soap star. Patrika is not your stereotypical glamour queen. She is a pretty woman, but stands five-feet-two inches and weighs about 200 pounds. Yet she was one of the most popular characters on the daytime drama *Days of Our Lives*, and got hundreds of e-mails each week. It's not hard to figure out why. Most women could relate to Patrika much better than to the other tiny, gorgeous women on the show.

That's not to say being overweight is a good thing. Patrika talked about how she continually tries to control her weight. But she made the point that it's only in recent history that skinny and beautiful were synonymous. Today's slender, "ideal" woman wouldn't have made it across the prairie in early America. Our society's view of beauty is unrealistic and can be very *un*healthy. I once talked with a young woman in her thirties who matter-of-factly said that when she was in college many of the girls tried extreme methods of staying skinny. She had experimented with laxatives and even purging, but just couldn't seem to get the hang of it. I was amazed that this Christian woman would have considered such unhealthy methods of weight control. But she didn't seem to think it was a big deal.

Anorexia and bulimia are rampant among women because they believe the lie that if they are slim enough, they will be beautiful, and people will accept and love them. Girls sometimes fall into these destructive behaviors before they even reach their teen years, and I believe television and movies are partly to blame.

We are bombarded with television commercials and programs that show women with perfect bodies, perfect skin, and perfect hair. And what about those size zero models with tiny hips, a tiny waist, and a *huge* bosom? Very few women are built like this, but we compare our shape to theirs and feel fat and ugly. We all but worship the human body. The Bible cautions us about worshiping the creature rather than the Creator (Romans 1:25).

If you obsess about your weight or body, I recommend you read Lisa Bevere's book *You Are NOT What You Weigh,* in which she shares about the years she was chained to the disorder of weight and food obsession. Lisa tried everything to be thin, including laxatives and purging, and was anorexic at times. When she was lonely, frightened, or bored, she went to food instead of God. But when she finally let Him fill the emptiness inside, she was able to change her lifestyle and maintain a healthy weight.

What are we mothers teaching our daughters about their bodies? Are we teaching them a godly view of beauty and health, or the world's view?

Focus on the Natural and Miss the Supernatural

Many Christians fall into conformity because they have become too earthly minded. While it's true we live on the earth and must deal with life here and now, we should guard against becoming so immersed in the *natural* that we miss the *supernatural.* The writers of the New Testament often refer to concepts of the Christian faith as a "mystery." They speak of the mystery of the gospel, the mystery of Christ and the church, the mystery of the kingdom of God, the mystery of God's will, and the mystery of faith, to name a few. These truths are a mystery because they are so diametrically opposed to what the world believes. They cannot be rationalized and explained.

Yet too many Christians have conformed to the point that we miss God's miraculous and mysterious intervention in our everyday lives. We say we know Jesus, but some of us wouldn't recognize Him if we bumped right into Him. That's what happened to Mary.

Mary Magdalene, who is mentioned more than any other woman in the New Testament, had a life-changing encounter with Jesus and became His devout follower. Mary had many wonderful qualities we can emulate — servanthood, faithfulness, and generosity. But she failed one big test.

Mary Magdalene was among the women who went to the tomb that Easter morning to embalm Jesus' body. When they saw His body was gone, they ran and told the disciples. The disciples came, but were baffled and went back to their homes — everyone, that is, except Mary. She was alone at the tomb weeping. I believe she was crying in frustration because she couldn't perform one last act of kindness on the body of her Lord.

Then Mary turned around and saw Jesus, but *she didn't recognize Him*. She thought He was the gardener. She said, "Sir, if you have carried him away, tell me where you have put him, and I will get him" (John 20:15). Mary was so immersed in the natural that she missed the supernatural. She had a head-on encounter with the greatest miracle in history — and she missed it!

How could she have spent the better part of three years working closely with this man and not recognize Him? Mary was there when Jesus healed the blind, opened deaf ears, and cast out demons. She was standing nearby when Jesus raised Lazarus from the dead. She was transformed as she listened to His teaching, though like the disciples, she didn't quite get it. Was it the early morning light or the tears in her eyes that kept her from recognizing the Lord? I don't think so. I believe Mary was blinded by her carnality. In her mind Jesus was dead, and she had moved on.

Whenever I read this story I can't help but wonder how many times we have missed the miracles God performs in our lives. Do we even recognize it when God answers our prayers? Do we recognize His protection and guidance? What blessings are we missing? How many times do we, figuratively speaking, come face-to-face with Jesus but see only the gardener?

As Christian women who want to resist temptation and live to please God, we must refocus our thinking toward heaven. "Since, then, you have been raised with Christ, set your hearts on things above, where Christ is seated at the right hand of God. Set your minds on things above, not on earthly things" (Colossians 3:1-2).

BUILDING SAFEGUARDS AGAINST CONFORMITY

In the Sermon on the Mount, Jesus makes clear that we are to be *in* the world, yet separate and different from it. He also told us, "You are the salt of the earth. But what good is salt if it has lost its flavor? You are the light of the world—like a city on a mountain, glowing in the night for all to see" (Matthew 5:13-14, NLT). He didn't isolate Himself from sinners and neither should we. So how, then, can we live as part of this world without being influenced by it? Here are some safeguards against compromising our standards and conforming to the world.

Adopt a Biblical Value System and Find Godly Role Models

When you know God's Word you can better resist the temptation to embrace the world's values. The Bible is the standard for the way we live—not the secular media or the politically correct worldview. If we don't know what God has to say, then any "truth" can sound reasonable. Many Christians are simply not equipped to distinguish between the truth and Satan's lies.

The Bible is clear on many issues, such as abortion, homosexuality, divorce, lying, occult activity, sexual immorality, and so on, but less clear on issues such as how we dress or what we should allow our kids to do. But the Holy Spirit will direct you if you sincerely desire to maintain godly standards. The key is to keep a sensitive conscience and pray about any activity you're not sure of. If you really want to resist the temptation to conform to the world's standards, God will let you know when you have stepped over the line into sin.

Godly role models can also help us resist conformity to the world. Think of a woman who has been an inspiration to you—someone who you think personifies the character of Jesus. I'm thinking of someone right now; her name is Sue. She is a woman of prayer and has been greatly used of God. I know that she loves me and has held me up in prayer for years. She is balanced and knows God's Word. If I have a question or concern, I can go to her and ask. Sue is someone I can emulate to help me live in the world, but not of the world.

Rather than comparing yourself with film and television stars or models, compare yourself with a godly role model. Instead of falling prey to the world's demands for perfection, focus on being healthy, exercising, eating good foods, and doing the best you can with the rest. "Charm can be deceptive and beauty doesn't last, but a woman who fears and reverences God shall be greatly praised" (Proverbs 31:30, TLB).

If you don't know someone personally, look to respected Christian leaders who have demonstrated over the years their godly character and wisdom in teaching other women. Read their books. Take part in their Bible studies. If you really want to live a holy life, it's not difficult to learn what God expects of you.

Connect with a Strong Christian Support Group

While we live and work surrounded by unbelievers, we need to spend a large portion of our time with people of faith. So take advantage of Bible studies and prayer groups, and get involved in your church. Those who share our beliefs and values can be our safeguard for resisting conformity. Spend time with them.

Yes, we should have unsaved friends and reach out to them, but we should be close enough to other Christian women that we can help each other resist the temptation to compromise. When you see a friend step over the line in her dress, habits, priorities, or spiritual health, pray about it *before* you say anything. Examine your heart to make sure you are not motivated by jealousy, envy, or some other wrong motivation. If your heart is right, go to her in love. We all need friends who will be honest with us because it's easy to drift away from God's standards.

Guard Your Finances and Your Priorities

In our affluent American society, it's easy to fall into the trap of placing too much importance on money and possessions. To determine where you might be vulnerable to temptation, ask yourself these questions:

- How do I view money and how does it make me feel? Is it a means to an end, or is money my goal?
- Am I living above my means?
- Have I allowed my career to crowd out other important things in my life?
- Do I feel I have to work outside the home and make a certain amount to be considered smart and successful?
- Have I been at peace or depressed during times of financial need?
- How much of my money do I give to God's work?
- How much do I give to others in need?

Be honest and use these questions to evaluate your priorities. Have you let the world's obsession with money creep into your heart? I recently attended a convention where I heard Chuck Colson, founder of Prison Fellowship, speak. He said that we in this country live by the lie that happiness is all about money and all about me. Chuck said we must live for others, and that we can only keep what we give away. He has spent his post-Watergate life giving of himself to prisoners all over the world. I challenge you to give *lavishly*. It will make you truly rich.

Expect the Supernatural

Do you catch yourself being cynical about the supernatural? Does the mystical side of Christianity make you uncomfortable? Do you rationalize or doubt the miracles of Scripture? Don't allow unbelief and a carnal mindset to rob you of the wonders of God. Look for His divine hand in your life continuously. Pray and *expect* an answer. Share testimonies of answered prayer with others and listen to their stories. Talk about and delight in the "mystery" of the things of God. Look for Jesus where others might only see the gardener.

Karen Mains has written a book called *The God Hunt*. Through her own experiences and the stories of others, she shows us how to find God in everyday living. She encourages us to see God's hand through such things as answers to prayer, evidences of His care, and strategic encounters.[4]

Don't become so ingrained in this earth that you miss those glimpses of heaven. Expect a miracle—and you just might get one.

You can use these safeguards to bolster your resistance to conformity and become a woman of character and conviction.

Becoming a Woman of Character and Conviction

The story of Ruth is an amazing portrait of a friendship. Perhaps you have admired Ruth's loyalty to her mother-in-law and enjoyed the incomparable romance that unfolds in the little book—as I do. But have you ever considered the temptations Ruth had to resist to make it all happen?

Naomi and her husband had moved to Moab from Bethlehem, along with their two sons. One of them married Ruth and the other Orpah, women who were not from their faith or culture. After a few years, Naomi's husband died and then she lost her two sons. The three widows were left alone.

It's understandable that Naomi would be grieving and at a very low point emotionally. She had lost her husband and both her sons. But she had also become bitter. "Almighty God has dealt me bitter blows. I went out full and the Lord has brought me home empty; why should you call me Naomi when the Lord has turned his back on me and sent such calamity!" (Ruth 1:20-21, TLB) She blamed God and thought He was punishing her.

Naomi decided to go back to Bethlehem to her own people. She told her daughters-in-law to return to their parents' homes and perhaps they would find new husbands. Orpah decides to take Naomi's advice, but Ruth refuses to leave her mother-in-law. In one of the most well-loved passages in the Bible Ruth declares her loyalty and love for Naomi.

> Where you go I will go, and where you stay I will stay. Your people will be my people and your God my God. Where you die I will die, and there I will be buried. May the LORD deal with me, be it ever so severely, if anything but death separates you and me. (Ruth 1:16-17)

Ruth must have been tempted to stay in Moab where it was familiar and safe. Why did she decide to travel to a strange land with a bitter old woman? Obviously, the women had forged a strong friendship and loved one another. But I believe it was because she had embraced Naomi's God. Ruth had come to believe the eternal truth about the God of the Jews, and to stay in an idolatrous nation would have been a huge compromise for her newfound faith. Perhaps she could have remained true to Jehovah in Moab. It was not a sure thing that she would turn her back on God. But Ruth refused to put herself in a position of vulnerability. What a lesson that is for us in setting our standards high and building safeguards to resist temptation. Ruth decided to do what she knew was right, even though others, even Naomi, encouraged her to take the easier road.

When they arrived in Judah, Ruth could have become bitter and had her own pity party. Instead, she set to work immediately, gleaning in the fields to support herself and Naomi. Here she was among strangers with not many prospects of finding a husband. She toiled all day in the hot sun to put food on their table. She could have succumbed to dissatisfaction, selfishness, envy, or strife. Like Naomi, she could have caved in to negativity. She could have compromised her standards and chased after young men. But Boaz later praised her for not doing that (3:10). This godly woman kept a good attitude, worked hard, and was faithful and obedient to Naomi and to God.

You know the rest of the story. Don't you love the plan Naomi came up with for giving Boaz the little shove he needed (Ruth 3:1-4)? It worked, and Boaz became Ruth's kinsman redeemer, portraying God's plan of Christ's redemption of the world. They were married, and Ruth gave birth to Obed. Naomi's grandson was a wonderful and unexpected gift to her, and his birth thrust Ruth directly in the lineage of David and Jesus Christ.

As Ruth's story illustrates, when we stand firm and refuse to compromise, we may have to make some sacrifices, but the rewards will be profound and eternal.

Ruth's Virtues We Can Emulate

- Loyalty to her family
- Faithfulness to God and others
- Diligence
- Unselfishness
- Modesty
- Humility
- Obedience
- Strong Convictions

It's not easy for Christian women to keep their standards high in the environment of today's world. It's human nature to blend in and copy the behavior of those around us. But women of godly character march to a different drummer. We follow a different set of rules.

Is your life a message to the world around you? If you want to live above compromise and conformity, simply ask yourself before every choice you make, "What would Jesus do?"

CHAPTER SIX:
MORALS, MONEY, MINISKIRTS,
AND MIRACLES

Study and Explore

The following Scriptures contain warnings or admonitions to help us resist conformity and compromise. Write a few key words of instruction beside each passage.

Example: Exodus 23:2 — Don't follow the crowd to do evil.

Leviticus 18:3-5

Job 27:6

Romans 12:1-2

Ephesians 6:10-18

1 Timothy 1:19

1 Timothy 4:1-2

Hebrews 10:23

1 John 2:15

Consider and Reflect

1. In what areas do you think a Christian should be different from the world?

2. In your opinion, what are some of the most common ways Christians compromise?

3. How much "tolerance" should we have? How can a Christian stand for righteousness without being judgmental?

4. How can we get a clear picture of the real character and nature of God?

5. Explain what it means to hate the sin but love the sinner.

6. If we believe the Bible is true, why is it difficult to recognize the supernatural in our day-to-day lives?

7. Reflect on your life. Have you been tempted to compromise in any of the following areas? If not, just leave it blank. Put a check by the ones where you've given in to temptation. Put a cross by the ones you successfully resisted.

Choice of friends and relationships

Entertainment

Politics

Finances and possessions

Sexual purity

Parenting
(Allowing excessive conformity
in your children)

Conversations

Off-color jokes

Church attendance

Reading materials

Manner of dress

Sexual fantasy

8. Ask God to show you why you yield to conformity and compromise. Could it be for one or more of the following reasons?

- Lack of relationship with Christ, possibly due to inadequate devotions, Bible reading, and prayer
- Misunderstanding of what God's standards are due to lack of Bible knowledge or erroneous teaching

- Love the things of the world more than God
- Lack the courage to go against the flow
- Fear that people won't like or accept you
- Fear your children will not like you or you won't be accepted by their friends
- Complacency
- Inability to resist the pull of your carnal nature
- Weak faith regarding miracles and the supernatural

Pray

Lord Jesus, show me every area of compromise in my life and forgive me for conforming to the world's standards. Give me a stronger desire to please You than anyone else. Give me the courage to do what is right, even when all those around me do what is wrong. Help me to be in the world without copying its ways. Allow me to keep a sensitive spirit regarding sin so I won't tolerate, ignore, or rationalize it. Give me wisdom in raising my children, so I might teach them strong moral values. Help me to know when to say "no" and when to say "yes." Help me to set my code of behavior in accordance with Your Word, not what is commonly acceptable. In Your name, Amen.

CONTROL FREAKS AND TEMPER TANTRUMS

The Temptation of Strife

It is better to live in a corner of the housetop than in a house shared with a contentious woman.

PROVERBS 25:24, RSV

llen was the director of special events for a Christian organization. Although she was very bright, she created strife wherever she went. She was insensitive to others; in fact, she used people as a means to an end. She was constantly offending those she worked with and created a contentious atmosphere both at the office and with outside vendors. Her employer continuously had to put out fires Ellen had caused through her aggressive nature. For instance, one time when Ellen was trying to get local pastors to announce an event at a retreat center in their churches, she was so pushy and aggressive that most of the pastors refused to work with her, and it ultimately hurt the success of the event.

Ellen was not only pushy and insensitive, she was also proud and egotistical and constantly complained that all her gifts and talents weren't being utilized. Eventually, her liabilities outweighed her assets, and her boss had to terminate her.

Of course, everyone is bound to create strife sometimes. But for women like Ellen, sowing discord is as natural as breathing. They can cause a stir by simply walking into a room, and the results can be heartbreaking. I have watched strife destroy marriages, friendships, churches, and women's ministries.

For this reason, I have worked diligently to bolster my own resistance to this temptation. Like many Cholerics, I have a quick temper and can get angry and contentious easily, yet my Sanguine part desperately wants to please. One of my hot buttons is when someone calls me down or criticizes me—especially my husband. When he criticizes me, a rush of emotions causes me to speak before I think—disappointment that I have failed to please him, anger that I have been unfairly treated, and fear that I don't measure up. When I lash out in anger, I've yielded to the temptation to cause strife.

What about you? Are you quick tempered? Do you get a little adrenaline rush when you prove someone wrong? Do you take pride in being able to express a strong opinion on almost any subject? If you answered "yes" to these questions, chances are you sometimes create an atmosphere of contention with those around you.

How Are We Tempted to Create Strife?

In order to help you recognize this temptation when it appears in your own life, let's look at the ways we create strife at home, in church, and on the job.

At Home

Our homes, especially our Christian homes, should be islands of peace in a world of chaos and hostility. Our husband and children should be anxious to rush home, knowing that when they arrive they can truly relax. Whatever challenges they faced at work or school can be forgotten at least for a few hours. But instead of making our home a refuge of peace, love, and harmony, we sometimes yield to the temptation to cause strife by greeting our children and husband with criticism, nagging, and complaining. We wives and moms are faced with a test every day: Will I create an atmosphere of love and harmony? Or will I contribute to the strife? It took me years to recognize one of these tests in my own life.

Jerry has never been good about picking up after himself—a habit I find annoying. He usually leaves a trail of keys, telephone, receipts, and glasses. What I find most challenging, though, is his tendency to leave his shoes and socks wherever he decides to shed them—in the family room by the television, beside the bed, or in his study.

I have tried everything to cure him. I have nagged and complained. I once threw his shoes and socks to the bottom of the basement stairs, hoping they would get a scratch or two—his punishment for not doing what I wanted. I have put his shoes and socks in the garage. I have even tried stuffing his dirty socks into his pillowcase! (I don't think he even noticed.) Nothing worked.

Several years ago I had a lightbulb moment. I realized this habit of Jerry's was a test—perhaps from God Himself. And I had failed. I had refused to give up control of my environment and had continued to fight my husband for my own way. While Jerry could have worked harder to change his ways, I knew he wasn't being malicious. He honestly didn't think about what he was doing. He had picked up the habit in grade school. But Jerry's failures weren't the point. This wasn't about my husband; it was about *me*.

I asked God to forgive me for letting such a small thing create strife in our home for so many years. I decided to accept this habit of Jerry's, change my attitude, and not let it affect my peace of mind. It was not worthy of one more battle. I have made peace with the shoes. Now I just move them to the laundry room, and about once a week I ask him nicely to take them to his closet. I still don't like seeing them, but giving up control has been good for me and my marriage.

Why do women yield to these temptations? I certainly didn't get up in the morning thinking of ways to make life difficult for my family—and you likely don't either—yet that is exactly what we do. Why does this happen?

One reason is that we let down our guard with those we love. We don't put on our best behavior for our loved ones. Instead, we give in to our weaknesses and character flaws and expect them to love us anyway. When we are with friends or at work or church, most of us make some effort to be agreeable, but at home we just are who we are—the good, the bad, and the ugly.

We fail to be affirming and kind. We fail to exhibit patience and consideration, because we can get rid of our frustration by being harsh or rude. We unconsciously punish our husband or children because someone (maybe even ourselves) or some *thing* has disappointed us. We can't direct our anger or frustration at an overdrawn checking account or a broken down car, so we transfer it to our husband or children—something we *can* control. We treat them in a manner we would never treat a stranger. We are unkind or demanding because it puts us in control again.

In *The Screwtape Letters,* C.S. Lewis has written an insightful, and at times amusing, study of the strategy of temptation through the eyes of Screwtape, one of Satan's chief demons. In the following passage Screwtape is suggesting to Wormwood, his demon protégé, ways of creating strife between a mother and son. He writes:

> When two humans have lived together for many years, it usually happens that each has tones of voice and expressions of face which are almost unendurably irritating to

the other. Work on that. Bring fully into the consciousness of your patient (the son) that particular lift of his mother's eyebrows which he learned to dislike in the nursery. . . . Let him assume that she knows how annoying it is and does it to annoy. . . . And, of course, never let him suspect that he has tones and looks which similarly annoy her.[1]

Screwtape obviously understood that the mannerisms and habits of those we love can grate on our nerves and tempt us to cause strife. That's the reason we cannot allow relationships to take their natural course. When we live closely with others, their flaws and bad habits annoy us, and vice-versa. That's why we must be proactive in *creating peace* rather than simply allowing potential conflicts to play themselves out.

Unfortunately, the temptation of strife can also be seen in our churches.

Within the Body of Christ

Pastor Don's church was large and doing well. He and his wife Linda were well respected in their community and popular with the folks in their congregation. Then practically overnight, something crept into their church that can only be called sinister. It began small but grew like a cancer—spreading slowly at first, then gaining momentum as the days and weeks went by. And like a dreaded disease, it resulted in much pain and suffering.

Don and Linda's lives were turned upside down by a handful of people who became disgruntled with Don as the pastor. At first they kept their complaints to themselves, but eventually sought out others who were unhappy. They decided they wanted Don and Linda out. They didn't find Don's sermons interesting enough, and they felt that Linda should be more involved in the church. They wanted someone younger, who would appeal more to young couples. Their criticism deteriorated into vicious lies and some people believed them. They rallied others to join them, and before long the congregation split into two factions. Don and Linda didn't want to be divisive; they hoped and prayed the situation would improve, but things only got worse.

Though it's difficult to believe, this pastor actually began to receive hate mail and death threats. Things got so bad that when Don and Linda walked into the church, these spiteful people would stand and hiss and boo at them. (Remember, this behavior wasn't happening with adolescents in the halls of a high school. It was in the house of God!)

Eventually Don was forced to resign. He took another pastorate, and about 150 members of his former congregation joined him at his new church. I'm sure it comes as no surprise that the old church immediately went into a decline that ultimately resulted in its total demise.

Did you recognize The Eve Factor at work in this church? The gossipers yielded to the temptation to listen to the Enemy. They probably believed the lie that they were protecting their church in some way by putting the "bad" pastor in his place. They chose to go against God's rules by gossiping and sowing discord among the believers, and finally—they convinced others to join in their sin.

Satan takes delight in creating division in a church or Christian organization through strife. It interrupts the ministry and distracts the leaders from doing their jobs. It can destroy the faith of new believers. Imagine the joy Satan feels when God's children make the family of God a place of dissension and strife. A place that should be an oasis to thirsty seekers can become a den of mistrust, gossip, jealousy, and competition.

The troublemakers can become so accustomed to this behavior, they don't even realize what they are doing. They might even couch their gossip and criticism in religious terms such as, "God spoke to me," "Someone needs to hold her accountable," or "I love them, but . . ." Whatever they might call it, creating strife is sinful and destructive. No wonder Paul lists contention, hatred, wrath, and strife as serious sins of the flesh, wedged in between idolatry, hatred, and murder (Galatians 5:20). Proverbs lists seven things God hates that are "an abomination" to him. One of these despised sins is "sowing discord among the brethren" (6:19).

Strife at work has a slightly different face than strife in the home or church, but the cause and effect can be similar.

In the Workplace

Some friction is inevitable at work because of the mix of personalities and temperaments. For instance, many CEOs are Powerful Cholerics who want to be in control. If a company is led by a Choleric Melancholy, it likely has a lot of turnover, because the person at the top is not only controlling, but also a perfectionist. When you throw into the mix the Phlegmatics, who can be slow moving and hard to motivate, and the Sanguines, who'd rather socialize and take long lunches than do serious work, you have a recipe for a lot of strife.

In addition, the politics and competition in many work environments can be brutal as workers compete for the boss's attention and approval, the next big promotion, or the juicy salary. Since it would be career suicide for an employee to yell, nag, or be openly critical (like we do at home!), we sometimes resort to gossip and complaining among ourselves. You may gripe to a coworker about being treated unfairly or having been passed up for a promotion. Or you might feel that because you *are* honest and have integrity, and have tried to act in a godly manner, others have taken advantage of you. It's a difficult pill to swallow and there is temptation to "get even." Resist it.

The workplace is perhaps our greatest opportunity to be salt and light in our world. It is an honor, as well as our responsibility, to show what a Christian acts like under pressure. If you must spend eight hours a day with nonbelievers, you can still be a light and an example of Christ's love. You can refuse to be a part of the gossip and backbiting. You can bring peace instead of strife to your job.

What would ever motivate us to create strife instead of peace? In order to resist this temptation, it helps to understand what lies behind it.

Why Can't We Just All Get Along?

I am not a therapist and do not claim to understand the psychological reasons a person might have a problem relating to others. Keep in mind that the following observations come solely from my study of Scripture and my experiences as a wife, mom, lay counselor, and person in ministry. I share them in hopes they may help you identify some reasons you might be creating strife in the lives of those around you.

Pride and Ego

Pride, the first sin recorded in history, is the granddaddy of all sin. Lucifer fell from heaven because of his pride. I like what Christian writer and pastor Rick Ezell has to say about pride:

> Pride, the antithesis of humility, is a spiritual cancer that eats away at our spiritual eyes, rendering us blind. . . . We cannot see our pride because we are so full of it. Pride is the spiritual veil that blinds us to the truth about ourselves and obscures our need for God.[2]

The arrogant, self-important woman alienates those around her. She believes she is always right, so others make a point of proving her wrong. Do you know a woman who fits this description? If so, you know that the conversation always has to be about her. She has all the answers. She is better at everything, and her children are perfect too. Those around her often retaliate by challenging, undermining, or maybe even secretly sabotaging her. Pride and ego are the enemies of peace, harmony, and loving relationships.

Even if we are not openly obnoxious, most of us have certain areas where we are vulnerable to this temptation and where our pride and ego show through. Let someone cast a shadow on that sensitive area, and we can react by getting our feelings hurt, pouting, or getting angry.

If your relationships are stormy, prayerfully ask yourself why. God can reveal your weaknesses in this area and the reasons you act and react the way you do. Perhaps you didn't grow up in a nurturing home where all your needs were met and you had to learn to be self-sufficient. Maybe you had to fight for everything, and you still cling to that method of survival. Perhaps you have been so hurt in the past that you've put up a protective barrier that comes across to others as arrogance. Or you may be more susceptible to pride because you were a spoiled, only child who grew up thinking you were the center of the universe.

Pride and ego must be eliminated from your life. The Bible is full of warnings about pride's destructive nature (see Proverbs 11:2; 16:5,18,28; 29:23). Pride is the most grievous sin, because it denies the need for God, the foundation for our relationship with Him. Every one of us needs to guard against the wicked lies of the Enemy, who would make us think we are sufficient in ourselves and superior to others.

Pride often results in an overly controlling nature, as they are closely related.

A Controlling Nature

Many moms have a need to control everyone and everything. It's a habit we easily fall into because it's our responsibility to guide our children, see that homework and chores are done, and monitor their time, activities, and friendships. But we must also give our kids freedom. As our children get older, they must learn to manage their own time effectively. But sometimes we moms get so used to calling the shots we have difficulty giving up control. This puts unnecessary stress on our children, and as they get older it can cause them to be angry, frustrated, and even act out in destructive ways. Colossians 3:21 says, "Fathers, do not provoke your children, lest they become discouraged" (RSV). A sure way to provoke children is for parents to try to control them.

I remember one incident with my oldest son, Jeff. He had done something to displease me and I lost my temper and was giving him a good tongue lashing. He answered me back in a manner I thought was disrespectful, so I told him in no uncertain terms to keep his mouth shut. He did so, but turned and gave me a look that would have wilted the flowers. This made me even angrier and I said, "And don't you dare look at me that way."

Jeff, in utter frustration, said, "Mom, when you talk to me that way, I can't retaliate or hit you. And then you won't let me explain my point of view or defend myself. And now you say I can't even look at you. What am I supposed to do?"

The truth of what he said stopped me in my tracks, and I was ashamed of myself and asked my son's forgiveness. Because I was the adult and Jeff was the child, I was trying to control him to the point of not allowing him to express his feelings in any way. I was abusing my parental status and causing anger and frustration in my son.

I learned a lesson that day, and in the future I tried to let my children express themselves and show their anger in an appropriate, respectful manner. Because we are bigger, stronger, and have authority over our children, we parents must be careful to resist the temptation to control our kids. Our efforts to control can easily turn into abuse.

If parents continue the pattern of control over adult children (and they often do), the children will separate themselves from the overbearing parents as quickly as possible, and may harbor bitterness toward them forever. They may be afraid to include the parents in their lives for fear they will keep trying to control everything, as they always have. No matter how difficult, we must learn when to take our hands off, zip our lips, and let our kids live their own lives.

If a woman is a control freak, she will not only try to control her kids, she'll also try to control her husband. Do you feel that when your husband arrives home his time is now yours? In the early years of our marriage, the minute Jerry walked in the door at night I would assault him with my grievances about the kids, or the bills, or a long list of things he needed to do. I finally realized I should give him some time to himself. After an hour or two, he was much more in the mood to talk, deal with the kids, or do what I needed him to do.

As a Choleric, I struggle with pride and a natural bossiness. If I let myself, I would tell Jerry when to go to bed and when to get up, how to load the dishwasher my way, and how to coordinate his clothes. (After all, I have a much better eye for fashion than he does!) Every day I have to resist the temptation to cause strife in our home through my controlling nature.

Fortunately, Jerry has a strong will and dominant personality much like mine. This mix, of course, causes conflict at times, but at least we balance each other pretty well. I pray every day for God to help me in this area, and I have seen improvement, but I will likely have to diligently fight this temptation for the rest of my life.

Be honest with yourself. Are you usually the one who picks the restaurant, the movie, the vacation spot, or the paint for the living room? The tendency to force your will on others is selfishness and pride at its worst.

Selfishness does not please God and will eventually destroy relationships. An agreeable husband may tolerate being dominated for a while. But the day will come when he'll retaliate. Either with explosions of anger and the accompanying fallout, or a passive-aggressive approach to getting even by withholding affection, being silent, or generally making his wife miserable. Or he could just walk out of the marriage.

We may also be more vulnerable to creating strife if we have unresolved anger.

Unresolved Anger

Anger is a natural human emotion. Jesus Himself was angry. The Bible tells us we can be angry without it becoming a sin (Ephesians 4:26). However, inappropriately expressed anger as well as repressed anger can be devastating to a relationship, whether it's a marriage, a friendship, or a relationship with a parent, child, or coworker.

If we have unresolved anger, we can injure others deeply with words spoken in anger, particularly if we express our anger through yelling and lashing out. Even if we apologize later, the damage can be irreversible. An angry woman can verbally (or physically) abuse children who can't really defend themselves. She may hurt others with her words because she wants to punish them for a hurt or violation she has experienced from someone else. The anger lies beneath the surface, just waiting for someone to set it off. We sometimes simply excuse it by saying we have a quick temper or a short fuse. Or we may not even realize it's there. That was the case for Karen, who I recently interviewed.

Karen was sexually abused as a child, and this led her into promiscuity early in her teen years. However, she heard something on the radio one day about sexual abuse and realized for the first time that she was a victim. She started going to church and became very devout, but she never talked with anyone who could help her heal from the sexual abuse. As a result, she had a lot of unresolved anger that she wasn't even aware of.

Then she met a wonderful young Christian man and eventually Ben proposed marriage. Before the wedding she told him about her past. She said, "I wanted him to know he was getting used goods." Ben said he loved her and didn't really care about her past, and they got married shortly after that. However, Karen's unresolved anger made her impossible to live with. She was continually lashing out at Ben and even rejected his love. Nor could she give freely of herself during sexual relations.

But then God did a miraculous work in Karen's life. One night lying in bed beside Ben, she earnestly prayed about why she was struggling. God showed her the underlying cause of her anger. She symbolically handed over her past hurts and anger to Him. In Karen's case, her life and marriage were dramatically changed. Though the anger occasionally surfaced, she was different from that day on.

For many women the healing from this kind of hurt happens gradually over time. If you are lashing out and hurting others, you need to identify what is causing your anger and find healthy ways to express it and eliminate it. As with Karen, honest, fervent prayer can bring complete healing. But especially in the case of abuse, professional counseling is often required.

Many women *repress* their anger or deny it, which can be just as harmful as expressing it inappropriately. Teacher and writer Mary Ellen Ashcroft observes that women are taught even as little girls not to fight or get angry. "When little boys are observed at play, they compete verbally and physically and fight. But little girls play cooperatively and try to resolve differences. As mothers we are always trying to cool the tempers of others. Therefore, it's hard for us to grasp that we can be good, Christian women and also get angry."[3]

We somehow believe we are not entitled to be angry, and think we are being weak Christians if we admit to genuine feelings of anger, hurt, or outrage when our rights are being violated. Of course we *do* get angry and the strife comes, because instead of expressing anger appropriately, some women suppress it and retaliate through passive-aggressive behavior. They withhold affection, are uncommunicative, uncooperative, pout, or push others away.

If we want to resist the temptation to cause strife, we must learn to communicate openly about our feelings—to our husband, to others, and even to God. He can handle it. It makes for much healthier relationships when a husband and wife can be honest and straightforward about their feelings and needs. Often the "silent and submissive" wife cannot even have a close, effective walk with the Lord, because her anger and frustration get in the way.

As Ashcroft points out:

> Anger seems to be miles from the submissive, servant-like ideal required of Christian women. . . . When we repress angry feelings we complicate the issues and add to our problems. Instead we need to look carefully at our anger, recognize what it is telling us and find healthy ways of dealing with it so that it doesn't turn into sin.[4]

When we refuse to let go of our anger, it will turn into bitterness. A bitter, unforgiving woman is certain to create strife, and will bring unhappiness to all her relationships. Be honest with yourself and ask God to reveal the weak areas that create strife, and then build the following safeguards to help you resist this temptation.

Building Safeguards Against This Temptation

Give Control Over to God

Most of us struggle with pride and the need to control at one time or another. For many of us, giving control over to God and others is difficult. But as we grow in our faith, we can learn to do this over time. Start with small things, such as allowing your children or husband to do things *their* way for a change. Ask God to give you a flexible attitude that allows others to make some of the decisions. Then try giving Him control of your finances or how you spend your time. Keep giving Him control, one area at a time. Eventually you can put your entire life into His hands—your will, your desires, your time, your ministry—everything.

Oh, I know pushy Cholerics like me will always be controlling, but we don't have to let it create strife. And we don't have to allow the temptation to become sin.

Find Healthy Ways to Get Rid of Anger

How can you deal with anger in a healthy way and not let it create strife? First, don't deny it. Do everything you can to identify the source and admit it. Talk to God about what is making you angry. He understands better than anyone.

Then get it out in the open. If possible, talk with the person or persons who have caused your anger. Share your feelings with them. If it's not possible to communicate directly with the person, talk with someone else about your feelings—a pastor or counselor. For example, when someone makes me angry, I will often discuss it with my husband. It helps me to verbalize my anger, and Jerry has a way of helping me put things in perspective.

Don't express your anger inappropriately or in a hurtful way. This can be a destructive habit that is hard to break. But with God's help you can learn self-control and healthier ways to express your anger. Here again, professional help might be called for.

Do what you can to let go of your anger. Give it to God. Resist the temptation to keep revisiting the hurt. Don't let the tape keep playing over in your mind or allow it to become hatred or bitterness. I know this is difficult, especially if you have been seriously hurt. But holding on to your anger only hurts *you*. With God's help it is possible to react to wrongs in a forgiving way that honors Christ. Forgiveness is a choice.

Remember the story about the disgruntled church members who caused a church split? Though it was a great tragedy, some good came of it. I know Don and Linda's adult daughter, Kathy, and they gave her a priceless gift as they demonstrated the godly way to react when others hurt or mistreat you. They responded with love and forgiveness and refused to criticize those who had created division. They rarely brought it up, refusing to rehash the wrongs done to them. Yes, they were angry about the way they had been treated. But they resisted the temptation to allow a harvest of bitterness. You can too.

Choose Peace Not Division

As women, we can either create a peaceful home or we can be the source of strife. Proverbs 19:13 sums it up pretty well. "A foolish son is his father's ruin, and a quarrelsome wife is like a constant dripping."

We often have no one but ourselves to blame for the contentious atmosphere in our homes. Our children certainly follow our example and often mirror our mood, tone of voice, and attitude as well as our actions — either for good or bad. When my kids were still at home I discovered that if I had a short, unkind manner with them, they took on the same rude manner. If I approach my husband with an argumentative or negative attitude, he will usually respond in kind. We can often change the environment for everyone by simply changing our attitude.

We not only set the tone of our household, we have the ability to *create* peace by being calm in the midst of chaos. We can help lower the decibel level by not raising our voice. We can teach our children to be polite and put others' needs before their own—even their siblings. We can *decide* not to nag or criticize or be argumentative (or let discarded socks and shoes bother us!). We can *decide* to speak kindly to family members and make sure our children do the same.

I strongly encourage you to determine *never* to take part in dividing the body of Christ. Guard those relationships more carefully than anything. Church and ministries are a fertile ground for the Enemy's temptations. He targets pastors and religious leaders. Guard against letting petty grievances cause trouble. Refuse to be a part of contention that can hurt God's kingdom. If you cannot help make peace, then back away.

Don't yield to the temptation to speak harshly or let petty irritations put a sting into your words, whether at home, church, or at work. While some of the strife in your environment may be beyond your control, you can refuse to be part of the problem. Not only that, you can proactively bring peace to those around you. That's what Abigail did.

Becoming a Peacemaker

The Bible tells us Abigail was beautiful *and* intelligent (1 Samuel 25). We don't have to read very far into her story to see how proactive she was in creating peace in a potentially volatile situation.

Abigail's husband Nabal, though extremely wealthy by the standards of the day, was an unbeliever, a scoundrel, and a fool. He was "mean and dishonest" (1 Samuel 25:3, NLT), so it's possible that he even mistreated his wife. What a mismatched pair! Abigail was poised, wise, smart, charming, and respected by the community and her own servants. But she often found herself having to cover for her boorish husband who was drunk much of the time.

Abigail is like many women I meet today. Though they may love their husbands, they cannot respect them and have to make the best of a difficult situation. They are faced with a test. Will they get angry, retaliate, lash out, and add to the strife in their home? Or will they look for ways to make peace? We cannot always control the actions of others who create contention. But like Abigail, we can usually find a way to make things better. Abigail chose to act as a peacemaker, though she had to use every ounce of creativity and cunning she had to prevent a disaster.

Nabal had once again lived up to his reputation and had insulted David and his men. David, who had been anointed as the next king of Judah, was not a man to be trifled with. Yet Nabal had refused to give David's men even meager provisions on a feast day.

When the men returned and told David what Nabal had done, he was furious. He gathered 400 of his men and rode out with the intent of destroying Nabal and his entire household.

When Abigail heard what had happened, fear gripped her heart. But she had a choice. She could be selfish and gather her children and flee to safety, leaving Nabal to get what he deserved at David's hand. Or she could attempt yet again to undo the mess her foolish husband had made. Abigail made the more difficult choice. She decided to reach out to her undeserving husband and try to protect her family.

So she sent David and his men gifts and provisions, and then she went out to meet David. She dismounted from her donkey, and bowed low, humbling herself before him. Her words present the perfect profile of a peacemaker.

1. Be willing to accept the blame.

Abigail started the conversation with an admission of guilt. "I accept all blame in this matter, my lord" (1 Samuel 25:24, TLB). Though the situation was not her fault, Abigail used one of the most effective strategies for creating peace. She took the blame. This is one of the fastest and surest ways to neutralize a volatile situation. When we assume blame it disarms our opponent by taking the fight right out of him or her.

We must be sincere, of course. But can't we, in most situations, honestly find some way we have contributed to the problem? By overreacting or being selfish? Instead of fighting to prove you are right, learn to take part of the blame.

2. Ask for and grant forgiveness.

Then Abigail asked forgiveness. "Forgive me for my boldness in coming out here" (1 Samuel 25:28, TLB). If accepting the blame is hard, asking for forgiveness can be even more difficult. Perhaps the most difficult words to utter are "I'm sorry, please forgive me." If we want to be a peacemaker, we must cultivate the art of asking for forgiveness and granting it to others.

Abigail was innocent, yet she asked David to forgive her boldness in approaching him. The strategy of asking for forgiveness, especially if we feel we are the injured party, is a discipline perfected over time. We resist asking for forgiveness because we don't want to admit guilt. But if we have accepted the blame, it makes sense to ask for forgiveness. And it is even more important to *be forgiving*. (Remember, one safeguard for preventing strife is to let go of your anger and refuse to become bitter.)

3. Find something positive to say.

Once Abigail had neutralized David's anger by asking for forgiveness, she proceeded to praise him. "The Lord will surely reward you . . . for you are fighting his battles; and you will never do wrong throughout your entire life" (1 Samuel 25:28, TLB). Nothing is more effective in diffusing anger and making peace than a well-placed compliment.

I wonder, how many wars and catastrophes throughout history could have been prevented by simple words of encouragement and affirmation? How many have been started by angry or careless words of criticism? A little stroking of the ego goes a long, long way to create peace. If we really try, we can always find something positive to say about others.

4. Appeal to reason and common sense.

Now that David's anger had subsided, Abigail could get practical. She appealed to his common sense, saying, "When the Lord has . . . made you king of Israel, you won't want the conscience of a murderer who took the law into his own hands!" (1 Samuel 25:31, TLB).

Abigail knew David would regret killing a whole clan of innocent people because of one foolish man's words. And she was right. David told her, "Bless the Lord God of Israel who has sent you to meet me today! Thank God for your good sense!" (verses 32-33, TLB). One way to keep strife out of your life is to figure out what's causing it and find practical solutions to solving the problem.

Abigail's Strategy for Making Peace:

- She was willing to accept the blame.
- She asked for and granted forgiveness.
- She found something positive to say.
- She appealed to reason and common sense.

Ask God to show you in what ways you are vulnerable to the temptation of strife, and why. Take an honest look into your heart and life. Is it pride, a controlling nature, anger, fear, or selfishness? Consider the words of Jesus:

> "Therefore, if you are offering your gift at the altar and there remember that your brother has something against

you, leave your gift there in front of the altar. First go and be reconciled to your brother; then come and offer your gift." (Matthew 5:23-24)

If you have strife in your life, consider your part in creating it. Ask God for wisdom and deliverance. Perhaps He will show you that you need professional help. Or maybe He will reveal your unresolved anger or controlling nature. Perhaps you need to develop self-control and healthy ways of expressing your anger.

You *can* move to a different place — a place of peace, newfound intimacy with God, and more harmonious relationships with others. It's never too late to become a peacemaker. Start today.

CHAPTER SEVEN:
CONTROL FREAKS AND TEMPER TANTRUMS

Study and Explore

Read the following passages and write down what each has to say about the *causes* or *consequences* of strife.

Proverbs 10:12
Proverbs 16:28
Proverbs 21:9
Proverbs 28:25
Proverbs 29:22
Mark 3:25
Ephesians 4:26
2 Timothy 2:23
James 3:14,16

Consider and Reflect

1. Other than her personality, what are three common reasons a person creates strife?

2. Can a woman who has a strong need to control her environment change and learn to be more of a follower? What are some suggestions you would give to help?

3. Why do pride and ego stir up strife? Why are they so offensive to God?

4. Do you have unresolved anger against someone? What are some steps you can take to express it appropriately and get rid of it?

5. Is an overinflated ego sometimes a front for feelings of insecurity? Can you think of someone in particular?

6. Would you consider yourself more aggressive or passive in temperament? What are some ways aggressive women create strife? What are some ways passive women create strife?

7. Think of some times you created strife unnecessarily in your home, church, or workplace. What was the outcome?

8. When you create strife and hurt others, do you feel remorse afterward? Do you push your guilt aside and act as though nothing is wrong? Or do you go to the people involved and ask for forgiveness? Think of specific examples of both.

9. Can you think of individuals right now who you should approach with an apology? Write down their names and pray for the courage and opportunity to make things right.

Pray

Lord Jesus, I accept the blame for causing strife in my life and the lives of others. Please forgive me. Help me to be honest with myself and reveal all those areas where I am failing You. Take away my pride, ego, and self-sufficiency and help me depend on You alone. Give me patience and self-control. Show me where my anger is coming from and help me get rid of it. Help me stop trying to control others and relinquish control of my life into Your hands. Help me to be a peacemaker. Give me the wisdom, determination, and discipline to do what I need to do. Where I am weak, help me to depend on Your power to change. Show me anyone I have wronged and give me the courage to ask forgiveness. In Your name I pray, Amen.

WHY DID I SAY "YES" TO THAT?

The Temptation of Overactivity

Never confuse activity with productivity.

RICK WARREN

I have sometimes watched in amusement a high-powered, multitasking woman at the mall. She has two children in tow and is pushing a third in a stroller. She has a hands-free phone headset and is talking a mile a minute. Her hands are shopping, her feet are walking, and she's settling disputes between the older children—all at the same time. I've always said a woman who can't multitask isn't worth her salt, but many of us get our lives out of balance through compulsive overactivity.

Of course, our lives can also get out of balance by doing too little. In the chapter on complacency we discussed the dangers of letting our spiritual life decline, failing to work on our marriages, not stepping out in obedience to God, and getting too comfortable with our blessings. This chapter deals with a life out of balance through doing too much.

Let me point out there is a difference between simply having too much to do and the temptation of *unnecessary* overactivity. You may truly have no choice but to be too busy. For example, if you are a single mom, you have to carry the load of two parents. You may be juggling a job, school, parenting, and church activities, and are unable to eliminate anything from your schedule. My heart goes out to all women in this place, and you are not the focus of this chapter. Rather, it is for those women who *could* keep their lives more in balance, yet they *choose,* either consciously or subconsciously, to be overcommitted and overinvolved to the detriment of their families, their health, and their peace of mind.

I know, because that was me until about fifteen years ago. I have been a Christian most of my life and have always been active in a church. I am fairly well organized, efficient, and have high energy. My activities have usually revolved around my church, ministry, and Christian friends. When my first two children were young, I worked off and on to help make ends meet, but when my third came along, I determined to be a stay-at-home mom. But as it turned out, I really didn't do less, I just did different things.

When the pastor's wife asked me to serve as the president of the women's ministries at my church, I thought, *Of course. My greatest passion is helping women, so this is a natural fit.* It was a demanding job. I spearheaded the monthly meetings and yearly retreats and the mother/daughter banquet for about 500 women.

I also led a weekly Bible study, sang in the choir and a women's trio, and was a part of the worship team. I also participated in the Easter and Christmas pageants, which involved at least half-a-dozen performances each season. These were the highlights of my year, especially if I got a speaking part or a solo. With all the weeks of rehearsals and performances, my family took a backseat during the holidays, and they ate a lot of fast food and TV dinners.

During this time my daughter was in elementary school and my boys were teenagers, so I volunteered as a room mother, helped with the high school youth activities at church, and participated in the parent-teacher organizations at their schools.

I also did a lot of carpooling. How I hated it! My stress level goes up just thinking about it. There was the day the car door broke as I was pulling out of the driveway and one of the kids had to hold onto it. And I still shudder every time I remember the morning I rolled over one of my young passenger's feet. Fortunately, he wasn't seriously injured.

For several years I had a home-based business as a color consultant and makeup artist. I had home parties during the day while the kids were in school or at night when Jerry was home.

I have always loved entertaining, so we often had employees or friends over for dinner. I still take great pleasure in a sparkling clean house, a beautiful table, soft music, and an impressive meal to serve my guests. Even though I was organized, things got pretty hectic just before the guests arrived, and I would be a grouch to Jerry and the kids. Then, when the guests began to arrive, I would turn into the charming hostess.

I did a lot of sewing and decorating back then and usually had a couple of projects going. I felt insecure about not having completed my college degree, so I also took a class or two almost every semester at a local college. In addition, I took some classes just for fun, such as calligraphy and tole painting. I took pride in giving my own unique creations for Christmas and birthday gifts.

Are you getting tired just reading about this schedule? I am. In fact, I think I'll take a nap! I did all that on top of the grocery shopping, cooking, cleaning, teacher's conferences, and hauling the kids to orthodontist visits, ball games and practices, and piano lessons. No wonder I lived on the edge of burnout.

But at the time I didn't realize how completely I had yielded to the temptation of overactivity. Were any of those activities wrong or sinful? Not in themselves, but when I was so busy doing things I didn't *have* to do that I was not able to take care of my husband and children well, I had crossed over the line. I was too exhausted to give quality time to Jerry or to be patient with the kids. I made my family miserable whenever we had guests because I wanted my dinner parties to be perfect. My priorities were misplaced and my life out of balance.

Can you relate to my story? Are your days so full of activity that they blur together like the landscape outside a speeding vehicle? Are you living on the edge of burnout? Is your life moving so quickly that you fear you are missing the best parts?

Being busy is good *as long as we are not tempted to be compulsive about it.* We can broaden our horizons, learn new skills, and grow through participation in many different activities and ministries. We can be a huge blessing to others and develop godly qualities in ourselves at the same time. But when activities start to push out the important things, such as quality time with family, time for building intimacy with the Lord, and taking care of ourselves, we have put activities before people and have yielded to temptation. When this happens we need to ask ourselves if we are trying to prove something or trying to fill an empty void in our lives.

What Makes Us Susceptible to This Temptation?

Why do we allow our lives to get so busy? I think it's likely a combination of factors including:

Temperament

Why did I knock myself out to participate in so many activities? Partly because of my temperament. The Choleric is the personality *most* susceptible to this temptation. We love to be busy and we *enjoy* working. We are usually high-energy and organized enough to handle a lot at one time. We often put unrealistic demands on ourselves and others, and easily fall into guilt when we don't feel we are accomplishing enough, which causes us to drive ourselves even harder. We find it difficult to relax, though we can be just as obsessive about hobbies and leisure activities as about work. We even plan every moment of our vacation, and tend to fill it with activity.

I am also Sanguine, so I was overly involved because the activities were fun! Music and drama allowed me to be on stage. I got to be noticed, wear costumes, sing solos, and be in front of hundreds of people every Sunday. I went out every week after choir practice and had a wonderful time with friends. My involvement was a way to belong and have close girlfriends. If someone had asked me at the time to keep only one activity, it would have been the choir. But that may not have been God's first choice for me.

Don't misunderstand. I am not apologizing for my Sanguine nature that loves being on stage or my Choleric nature to be highly productive. God made me this way. Today, I am on television and step onto a stage frequently to speak to women. I love it. God has certainly let my natural gifts play themselves out. But I should have made better choices that kept my life more in balance.

If you are one of the other two temperaments, your life can get out of balance as well, but for different reasons. If you are a Melancholy, you may take on too much work because you want to be perfect. While Phlegmatics aren't likely to struggle with doing too much, their problem may be doing too little, which also results in a life out of balance.

Need for Approval

This topic has appeared in almost every chapter of this book as a reason we are vulnerable to temptation, including unhealthy comparison, negativity, conformity, and others. It is also a major cause for overextending ourselves and saying "yes" to too many things. When we are driven to prove ourselves worthy and have a deep need to impress others and be admired and loved, it's easy to do too much.

Our need for approval causes us to tell ourselves, *Yes, I can serve on that committee (they will see what good ideas I have). I think I'll sign up for those classes (I can tell people I'm working toward my degree). Yes, I'll help with the ladies' tea (Sarah is in charge and I would love for her to notice me and be my friend).*

We think, *If I could only get that job, it would prove how smart and capable I am. If I could get that book or article published, then I'd know I really am a good writer. If I become president of the women's group, then God will surely be pleased with me.* We are driven to perform because we think the more we do, the more valuable we must be.

But no matter how much we do, our need for approval doesn't go away. We just get caught up in frantic, exhausting tasks, missing what's truly important and missing God's plan and calling for our lives. That's exactly what Satan wants us to do.

The Enemy

Satan will do whatever it takes to get God's people off track from the truly important things. He excels in causing us to focus on the trivial rather than activities with eternal value.

Here are some examples of how he works:

- You make a renewed commitment to early morning quiet time with God, and your daughter will suddenly have to be at school two hours early for cheerleading practice.
- You and your husband carve out an evening a week for your date night, and his boss suddenly requires him to work late.
- You grow closer to the Lord and see a real breakthrough spiritually, and all hell breaks loose in your household—literally.

Whenever we want to promote God's purposes and draw closer to Him, the Enemy will bring opposition through more hours on the job, house guests, demands from the children, or the family dog—anything he can use to distract us. He knows how easy it is to keep us from fellowship and intimacy with God through busyness. We must guard our hearts and our time carefully and be honest about the activities that fill our lives. Ask yourself, "Could some of the worthwhile things that keep me so busy really be temptations from the Enemy?"

Satan wants us to succumb to the temptation of overactivity because he knows a life out of balance is a life that misses God's best. Misplaced priorities will leave our children and our husbands with the short end. Satan knows if he can keep us busy enough doing *good* things, we will miss the *best* things—those that bless others and use our gifts to the fullest for God's kingdom.

How does this temptation play itself out in our lives? Let's examine how we fall into the trap and some of the fruits of overactivity.

How Do We Succumb to Overactivity?

Saying "Yes" to Too Much Religious Activity

Many of us can get too busy because our sincere desire to serve God prompts us to say "yes" to too many worthwhile activities. The old saying among preachers, "I'd rather wear out than rust out," certainly resonated with me. I wanted to work for the Lord. I loved women's ministry and Bible studies, and so I said "yes" to every opportunity to do those things. I believed the lie that said, "It's okay that your life is crazy. Don't worry about not spending time in prayer and devotions. Don't worry that you are too tired for sex. You are doing this for God." I assuaged my guilt by telling myself that although my personal time with God was almost nonexistent, *surely working for the music department and women's ministry counts for something.* We must guard against overextending ourselves with religious activity because we are trying to "earn" God's love and acceptance. He loves us anyway—even those who tend to do too little.

Valuing Activities More Than People

One of the fruits of overactivity is putting tasks before people. When I gave lovely dinner parties, I thought I was serving people—even though I was a grouch to my family. But I was actually trying to make myself look good at others' expense. If I had kept my focus on my primary calling at that time—to be a wife and mother—I probably wouldn't have been women's ministries president or involved in our church's music and drama programs or in leading worship. Or maybe I would have chosen to do only one or two of those activities.

From a grandmother's point of view, I now realize how fleeting the time is when our children are young or in their teens. I wish I had focused more on my children and my husband and had fewer outside responsibilities. I thought at the time my motives were honorable. But now I realize I was being selfish.

We must examine our motives and ask ourselves, "Is my busyness about *helping* people or about *using* people to make me feel good about myself?" Many women busy themselves in charitable causes, fund-raisers, and even commendable volunteer work for the wrong reasons. We can be involved in activities that ultimately contribute to helping people, but when we place more importance on those worthwhile activities than on our primary relationships, our lives are out of balance, and those close to us can suffer.

Allowing Our Kids' Activities to Dominate Our Life

Sometimes the problem isn't overinvolvement in activities *we* want to do, it's overinvolvement in activities our kids want to do.

I have talked to mothers who needed a computer program for keeping their children's schedules—soccer, gymnastics, Scouts, sleepovers, library, music lessons, and play dates. While our focus should be on our kids while they are growing up, that doesn't mean we should allow their *activities* to dominate our lives.

Not only can their activities cause our lives to get out of balance, if we let our kids get too busy, we are cultivating a habit of busyness in our children that may cause them to struggle in this area as adults. The best time to help them learn to keep their life in balance is when they are young.

We also need to be honest about why we want our kids to do certain activities. Is it truly something that would be good for them? Or are we encouraging the activity because we think it will make *us* look better?

Getting Our Priorities Out of Order

Getting our lives out of balance may be the result of simply making the wrong choices about how to use our time and getting our priorities mixed up. There are only twenty-four hours in a day, and at least a few hours of them we are sleeping. So how do we divide those other hours to be pleasing to the Lord and more beneficial to ourselves and others? Do we spend our time wisely—or do we waste time?

We all have to spend some time on repetitive tasks that keep our households and lives running—such as grocery shopping, cooking, cleaning, and paying the bills. But are we wasting time on repetitive, mundane activities? Are you a perfectionist and not flexible enough to perform necessary tasks adequately but *quickly*?

Some of us compromise our health by adding stress through unnecessary activities. We must balance our lives by having rest and leisure activities, but here again, *balance* is the key. It doesn't mean spending many hours each week vegging out in front of the television or reading newspapers or magazines or blogging on the

Internet. Only you can judge how to divide your time wisely. But ask yourself which activities are stealing valuable hours that could be spent doing something significant.

So, how can we resist the temptation to do too much? Here are some ways we can divide our time in a way that's pleasing to God and healthy for our relationships and our bodies.

SAFEGUARDS FOR KEEPING YOUR LIFE IN BALANCE

If your life is out of balance, you need to reorder your priorities. Here are some suggestions for discerning the truly important things over the trivial.

Put God First, People Second — Including Yourself

The Pharisees wanted to trick Jesus into saying something derogatory about the Law of Moses. So they asked Him what the greatest commandment was, and Jesus told them, "'Love the Lord your God with all your heart and with all your soul and with all your mind.' This is the first and greatest commandment. And the second is like it: 'Love your neighbor as yourself'" (Matthew 22:37-39). Then Jesus went on to say, "All the Law and the Prophets hang on these two commandments" (verse 40).

If we truly put Jesus first in our lives and love Him completely, we will keep our priorities in order. We will spend time in prayer, Bible reading, meditation, worship, repentance, and listening to the Holy Spirit. We will do whatever it takes to please God and show Him our love. Conversely, if we don't keep these priorities first, then we don't truly love the Lord as we should.

Jesus knew these commandments even superseded the Law of Moses. He knew those who loved God with all their hearts would not be putting other gods before Him or making graven images.

And Jesus' second commandment took care of the rest of the Ten Commandments. If we love our neighbors as ourselves we won't steal from them or murder or covet or lie. The entire Law rests on these two commandments, and they are the best measure for living a balanced life. Jesus wisely included "as ourselves" because He knew we needed to take care of ourselves in order to be able to love others as we should.

In chapter 4 I suggested that we be diligent in taking care of ourselves as a way of building a safeguard against complacency. Both *complacency* and *overactivity* can cause us to neglect our physical, emotional, or spiritual health. When our lives get out of balance, we often neglect our own needs.

So take a little time every day for yourself. I know that's difficult, especially if you have small children. But even fifteen minutes spent taking a bubble bath, or reading a good book, or polishing your nails can be healing. Such mini-vacations are critical if you want to keep your life in balance.

In addition, make your family and friends a priority over activities. Take the time to communicate with your husband and show him love and attention. Listen carefully when your children try to talk to you. Don't allow your mind to drift to other things or brush your kids aside. Give thoughtful answers to their questions. Take time to give that hurting friend a call rather than telling yourself you're too busy and putting it off until tomorrow.

Limit Your Children's Activities

Refuse to be in bondage to your children's schedules. Prayerfully and carefully decide together as a family which activities are beneficial and then choose only one or two.

If you spend most of your week running your children all over town, either cut out something or trade off with other mothers. Help small children learn time management by scheduling their day to include several different tasks such as devotions, play, reading, helping others, doing chores, and so on. If you're pushing your kids to be too involved, search your heart and ask God to show you what motivates you to push them, and then ask for His help in dealing with it.

Spend Less Time on Necessary Activities

You can also learn how to do necessary tasks and activities more efficiently. Get a handle on how you spend your time by keeping a log or diary of your daily activities for a week or even a month. This is the best way to see where your time goes, especially if you don't work outside the home. How much time are you spending doing housework and cooking? How many hours do you spend shopping for clothes or other personal items? How much of your time is spent on decorating your home? How much time do you spend in church, prayer, Bible study, and meditation? How much quality time do you spend with your husband? Helping others? In front of the television? How much time are you in the car running your children all over the place?

It could be you are too busy because you simply don't manage your time efficiently. There are many helpful books available on time management and organization, but here are some basic ways to limit the time you spend on necessary activities.

- Simplify your holiday celebrations. Take Christmas, for instance. Who says you need to bake hundreds of cookies for the holidays? Make a few dozen—or none at all. Buy simple, inexpensive presents. We all love to give and receive homemade gifts, but don't feel you're locked in to that tradition every year. Focus on creating lasting memories with your family. Make Christmas a celebration of Jesus' birth—not a stress-filled season of frantic overactivity.

- Simplify meals and dinner parties. Your trademark might be baking from scratch, but it may be a better use of your time to buy something from a bakery or choose a simple dessert. It's more important to spend the afternoon with your daughter or granddaughter baking cookies than to create a dessert masterpiece while she watches a movie alone.
- Choose easy, fast, familiar recipes. If your focus is on enjoying your guests and family and making them feel special instead of impressing them, it relieves a huge part of the pressure and stress.
- Simplify personal grooming. Granted, this gets harder as we get older, but don't let your health and appearance suffer because it takes too much time out of your day. Find an easier, less time-consuming hairstyle. Streamline your makeup application. Use neutral makeup tones that go with everything. Organize your closets, drawers, and jewelry. Group your skincare products for quicker morning and evening beauty regimens.
- Simplify healthy habits. I have joined a women's exercise franchise that offers fun, quick, and simple activity that is highly effective. I go three times a week for thirty minutes, and the facility is just a few minutes from my home. If it weren't quick and easy, I probably wouldn't exercise regularly. I have also found a health drink that includes all the nutritional supplements I need in one eight-ounce drink.[1] If I had to take handfuls of different pills at various times of the day, I wouldn't do it. But this drink provides a simple, quick solution to nutritional supplementation, something I feel is essential for my health.
- Simplify housework. If efficient housecleaning is not your strong suit, find someone who can teach you quicker methods and helpful tricks for grocery shopping, making beds, folding sheets, organizing papers, and so on. Would it work

to change your sheets every *other* week instead of every week? Could you do laundry only once a week instead of three times a week? If you can find a way to afford it, hire some help once or twice a month. Spend as little time as possible on the tasks that must be done over and over again. Every moment is valuable—and not just in dollars and cents.

- Don't demand perfection. Be flexible about the way you do things. Stop worrying if your house isn't spotless or your dinners spectacular. Perform for an audience of one—God Himself. You can't do everything perfectly, so cut out the fluff and focus on the activities with eternal value.

When you simplify the mundane yet necessary tasks, you have more time to devote to what God has called you to do—that which brings significance and purpose to your life. The next step is to determine exactly what that is.

Find God's Will for Your Life and Focus on That

Rick Warren reminds us that knowing our purpose helps us determine which activities are essential and which aren't. He suggests we ask ourselves, "does this activity help me fulfill one of God's purposes for my life?" He says:

> It is impossible to do everything people want you to do. You have just enough time to do God's will. If you can't get it all done, it means you're trying to do more than God intended for you to do (or, possibly, that you're watching too much television).[2]

What are your gifts? What are you best at? I enjoyed watching our three children grow up. Trevor was a social animal and had a gift for sales. When he was twelve, he was selling newspaper subscriptions door-to-door and made enough money during the summer to buy a nice pair of snow skis. Jeff couldn't have sold an overcoat to an Eskimo, but he loved reading and languages and had a keen interest in the Middle East. Vanessa always wanted to be a mother. She talked of little else. Today Trevor has his own business in sales and marketing. Jeff is in a Ph.D. program and teaches Hebrew. Vanessa has five children and is one of the most diligent, successful mothers I know. My children were fortunate because they recognized their gifts early and have focused their energies on them.

Most of us can do at least a few things well, and God's perfect plan for our lives usually includes some area of our giftedness. You may be spinning your wheels and wasting time because you have not yet determined what your focus should be. If you don't know what your strengths are, get your hands on some of the tests and books available that can help you determine your purpose and gifts. One such book is *What Color Is Your Parachute?* by Richard Nelson Bolles (Ten Speed Press). Another valuable resource is the "Uniquely You" materials that can help you determine your areas of giftedness (www.uniquelyyou.com or 1-800-501-0490). Ask God to help you determine His will and purpose for your life. Take into account which activities make you feel stressed, angry, or frustrated and which activities leave you feeling peaceful, happy, and closer to God? He may not show you His plan for the next five years or even next year, but He will help you focus your attention on the most important things *today*.

There is one woman of Scripture who can inspire us all to choose the *best* things over the *good* things and devote our time and lives to serving God.

Becoming a Woman Devoted to God

Mary and Martha lived in Bethany with their brother Lazarus. They were close friends of Jesus and His disciples, who often visited in their home. The most popular account of Mary and Martha is found in Luke 10:38-42 (TLB).

> As Jesus and the disciples continued on their way to Jerusalem they came to a village where a woman named Martha welcomed them into her home. Her sister Mary sat on the floor, listening to Jesus as he talked.
>
> But Martha was the jittery type and was worrying over the big dinner she was preparing.
>
> She came to Jesus and said, "Sir, doesn't it seem unfair to you that my sister just sits here while I do all the work? Tell her to come and help me."
>
> But the Lord said to her, "Martha, dear friend, you are so upset over all these details! There is really only one thing worth being concerned about. Mary has discovered it—and I won't take it away from her!"

Jesus gently rebuked Martha, not because what she was doing wasn't important. But Jesus probably knew this was a pattern in Martha's life. She was a *compulsive* doer. Hers is a classic story of a woman getting too busy—even though she was doing something worthwhile. Martha was a Powerful Choleric. Notice the telltale characteristics:

- The house belonged to her.
- She was organizing the party.
- She was hands-on and task-oriented.
- She was demanding.
- She had a difficult time sitting still and listening.
- She got her priorities out of order.

Jesus' words to Martha are a poignant warning for those of us who are more comfortable with *doing* than with sitting and listening.

Mary, on the other hand, was probably a Peaceful Plegmatic with a healthy dose of Melancholy thrown in. She much preferred listening over working, and her sensitive nature caused her to appreciate the profound teachings of Jesus. She couldn't have cared less about the dinner being prepared when matters of eternal importance were being discussed. But it was more than her temperament that caused Mary to pause and listen to the teachings of Jesus. She knew how to keep her priorities in order. She was a woman devoted to God.

There are other accounts of these sisters in the gospels that only reinforce their differences. Both sisters had qualities we can admire and emulate, but in Jesus' words:

> "There is really only one thing worth being concerned about. Mary has discovered it—and I won't take it away from her!" (Luke 10:42, TLB)

In John 12, Jesus and His disciples were again in Bethany visiting Mary, Martha, and Lazarus. Once again, Martha is serving—no surprise there. But this time, Mary takes an expensive vial of perfume and breaks it. The room becomes heavy with the sweet-smelling fragrance as Mary anoints Jesus' feet with it and wipes them with her hair.

Given Mary's temperament, this showy display may have been a little out of her comfort zone, but she loved her Savior. She loved Him with *abandon,* and all she cared about was worshiping Him. Many of us are so task-driven, we have difficulty loving Jesus with abandon.

What can we learn from Mary that can teach us to become women who are devoted to God above everything else? She loved Jesus and wanted to spend time with Him more than anything. She realized that listening to Him was the most important activity she could choose. She didn't let earthly demands crowd out heavenly concerns. She gave Jesus her most expensive gift, and she gave it *lavishly* for everyone to see. Could it be the most precious gift we have to give Jesus is our time?

Mary's Example of a Devoted Life

- She loved Jesus enough to spend time with Him.
- She didn't let earthly demands crowd out heavenly concerns.
- She gave her most precious gifts to Jesus.
- She discovered the one thing that was truly important.

Mary discovered the "one thing worth being concerned about." You can too.

Don't be a Martha who lets worthwhile tasks crowd out the best and truly important things. Structure your life based on the big picture, not just on today's to-do list. When you do, you will be a beautiful blending of Mary and Martha and will have time to enjoy the blessings of God.

Guard your priorities by giving most of yourself to God and His calling. Give a generous portion of what's left to your neighbors—your husband, your children, your friends, your church, and your coworkers. And guard at least a little piece of what's left for you. Ask yourself, "Will the things that fill my time seem important five years from now? Will someone's life be changed due to the activities I have chosen? Will heaven take notice? God will guide you if you slow down—take a deep breath—and call on Him for wisdom. When you prayerfully get your life in balance, you will *feel God's pleasure* in the things that fill your *time* as well as your *heart*.

CHAPTER EIGHT:
WHY DID I SAY "YES" TO THAT?

Study and Explore

Read Matthew 6:31-33. What do these verses say to you about priorities?

Read the following verses and write down how Jesus spent His time.

Example: Mark 1:35 — got up very early to pray

Mark 6:46

Luke 5:16

Luke 6:12

Luke 9:18

Luke 9:28

Read Jesus' parable in Luke 14:16-24. What is the message here about being too busy?

Consider and Reflect

1. In Luke 10:38-42, why did Jesus rebuke Martha?

2. What were some of Martha's strengths? Her weaknesses?

3. What were some of Mary's strengths? Her weaknesses?

4. Read the story of Mary and Martha in John 12. How do you explain Mary's behavior? Do you think Martha would have done the same thing? Why or why not?

5. Read Matthew 22:36-40. Explain how these verses can be used to establish priorities in our lives.

6. Why does this commandment supersede all of the Ten Commandments?

7. Is giving our time to God as important as giving Him our money? Which is easier to do and why?

8. Do you consider yourself more like Martha or Mary? Why?

9. Do you have a difficult time saying "no" when asked to do something? Why or why not?

10. If you are overly busy, consider whether you enjoy or dislike the frenetic pace. Examine your motives. What might you be getting out of it? Do you try to find self-worth through how much you can accomplish? Do you encourage your children to be too busy because you feel more successful and valued through their accomplishments? Have others put pressure on you to be too busy?

11. Make a list of the activities that make you feel happy, peaceful, and fulfilled. Now make a list of those that leave you frustrated, exhausted, or depressed. Though we all have to do things we don't particularly like, see if there are ways to reduce the stress in your life by spending less time on the distasteful tasks.

12. Check the areas that need more of your time in order to get your life in balance:

- Intimate, quality time with God including Bible study
- Concentrated effort to love, honor, and respect your husband
- Taking the time to nurture your children, to teach them spiritual truths, and to guide them toward living more balanced lives
- Mentoring others and developing close friendships
- Reaching out through the church and community to help others in need

Pray

Dear Lord, I admit to sometimes falling into the trap of compulsive busyness. Show me why I do this. Help me to know when to say "no" even to worthy, honorable tasks if they are not in Your plan for me. With Your help, may I get my life in balance and remember what You said about the "one thing that is important." Help me to step back and see my frantic schedule from a heavenly perspective. Give me the discipline and wisdom to reorder my priorities and focus on activities with eternal value. Make my motives pure and pleasing to You. In Your name, Amen.

LEARN TO HATE, FALL IN LOVE, AND WIN

Overcoming The Eve Factor

*As long as I remain under the refuge of innocence,
I am living in a fool's paradise.*

OSWALD CHAMBERS

A few years ago I was sitting in choir practice on Thursday evening. The director had just asked everyone to bow their heads for an opening prayer. My contacts had been bothering me, so I quietly opened my purse to take out my "tears in a bottle." I squeezed a few generous drops in my right eye, and instantly realized I had done something really stupid. I had grabbed the superglue instead of my wetting solution and was now in excruciating pain. My reflex was to put my finger to my eye, and as a result my eye glued shut and a tiny portion of my upper cheek bonded to my eye as well. I tapped my friend Bernie on the shoulder and ran out of the room in a panic. Bernie's a nurse, so when she discovered my problem she rushed me to the car and on to the emergency room of a nearby hospital.

The chemical in the glue was not only causing an intense burning sensation, but the glue had instantly hardened my contact into a jagged, contorted blob that was cutting my cornea. Needless to say, I was in bad shape when we arrived at the ER.

The young resident first used acetone to unglue my cheek from my eye, then pried open a tiny slit between my eyelids into which he poured anesthetic. The pain subsided considerably, but it took him about two hours to open my eye and remove the remains of the contact. Fortunately, although my cornea was scratched from the jagged edges, my eye was not seriously injured. Eyes heal quickly, so in a couple of days I was just fine.

The next morning when I went to an ophthalmologist, he told me I was the *tenth person* he had treated that year who had mistaken super-glue for contact solution and filled her eye with it. It made me feel better to know I wasn't the only one who had made such a dumb mistake.

Let me assure you—we all make mistakes. We all make bad choices and do foolish things. And, sooner or later, we all yield to temptation. It's difficult to have to face up to our mistakes. But Oswald Chambers' quote at the beginning of the chapter cuts right to the core of this book. I for one don't want to be in the dark about my sin, thinking all is well with my soul, when I am really living in a fool's paradise.

As you have read this book, you've likely seen yourself in several places—or perhaps only a few. But as Rick Warren says, "A little sin is like being a little pregnant. It will eventually show itself."[1] How true that is, and these chapters have covered a virtual catalog of temptations—a long list of *don'ts*.

But I have great news! This final chapter contains encouragement and practical helps for living a holy life that is truly pleasing to God. No more *don'ts,* I promise. Here you will only find a list of *dos.*

CONFESS YOUR SINS

God's nature is one of longsuffering, patience, forgiveness, and unending love toward us. John tells us, "If we confess our sins, he is faithful and just and will forgive us our sins" (1 John 1:9). To live a life pleasing to God, you don't have to be perfect, but you do have to learn to confess and repent of your sins quickly.

David was a man after God's own heart — not because he didn't make mistakes, but because he had a heart sensitive to his own failures. When he recognized his sin, he went to God with earnest repentance. God can use a person like that. He can handle any nasty sin we might commit. (David's was pretty horrible.) He *can't* handle it when we hide and try to cover our sin. It's as ridiculous as Adam and Eve trying to hide from the Almighty behind a bush. I would guess the most loathsome aspect of The Eve Factor in God's eyes is our trying to rationalize or cover our sin.

When we confess our sins and ask for forgiveness, we take the rug out from under Satan, who likes to accuse us before God and also to ourselves. When we don't confess our sins, we can live under a cloud of guilt, wanting to serve God but feeling we are hopeless failures. Satan makes us feel worse through his accusations.

Jerry experienced this when he found out he had cancer. The Enemy told my husband he was ill because he had failed God. He reminded Jerry of every sin, every failure, and every inadequacy. He tried to convince him he was of no more good to the kingdom and so God was casting him aside. For a time it was devastating. Jerry finally got victory when he said to Satan, "You're right. I *am* a sinner. I am far from perfect. I make mistakes all the time. But that's why Jesus died. All my failures and sins are under His blood."

When the Enemy's accusations hit you below the belt, don't despair. Consider this:

> Satan's accusations carry a certain amount of sting because they usually carry a certain fraction of truth. . . . Confess your sin, call it in its worst terms, and repent of it. So what if it's the umpteenth time? I know who I am.

I am not a sinner who struggles to love God; I am a lover of God who struggles with sin. I am primarily a lover of God, not a sinner.[2]

There is freedom in getting your temptation or sin out in the open. If I had kept my jealousy of Tammy and Michelle a secret, I might not have been able to get rid of it so quickly. I decided to confess my jealousy in a most unusual way.

The producers of my show decided to do a program on secrets and asked each of the cohosts to share a confession with a live audience. Since I'd just had a revelation about my jealousy, I thought it would be an appropriate, yet scary secret to share.

I couldn't believe how nervous I was. My mouth was dry and my palms were sweaty. If I hadn't been obligated to follow through with the show, I'm not sure I would have had the courage to face Tammy and Michelle.

Well, after my very public confession, I was diligent about searching my heart and keeping my attitude toward them pure. God has helped me, and I no longer experience any feelings of jealousy toward them. But I wonder, if my secret hadn't been made so public, would I have yielded to the temptation at a later time?

If you're struggling with temptation, find someone you can talk to. Ask your husband or a close friend to hold you accountable regarding the sins you are prone to commit. Be willing to own up to your mistakes, both to God and to others.

I recently interviewed a psychologist on the topic of addiction. He reminded the audience that in order to be free, an addict must *embrace* her addiction. Not in the sense that she *likes* it, but that she admits her problem, claims it as her own, stops blaming others, and moves forward in overcoming it. Don't hesitate to *confess* your *mess*.

ASK FOR HELP

It's not enough to admit our struggles and weaknesses to ourselves and to God, we must ask for His help. When we do, He will show us a way to resist the temptations we are susceptible to (1 Corinthians 10:13-14). Sometimes we have the strength of will and convictions to walk away from temptation on our own, but most of the time we need supernatural help.

My husband sat before a panel of university professors as he underwent an oral examination for his communications degree. In one of his responses Jerry used the term "Christian counselor." Immediately one of the professors asked, "What do you mean by a *Christian* counselor? What's the difference?"

Jerry said, "A counselor uses the sum total of all her knowledge, her education, what she has learned from others, her talents, abilities, and her experience to help her clients. A *Christian* counselor uses the sum total of all her knowledge, her education, what she has learned from others, her talents, abilities, and her experience. But when she reaches the end of all her resources, she can then call on Almighty God, the Creator of the universe, who has all knowledge, ability, and wisdom to help those in need."

When you're faced with temptation, you may feel powerless to say "no" even if you want to. But, guess what? God has unlimited power and resources, and He can give you the strength you don't have. He can use all the power in the universe if need be, and He *will* help you if you only ask.

Others in the body of Christ can also help, too. Rick Warren points out, "If you're losing the battle against a persistent bad habit, an addiction, or a temptation, and you're stuck in a repeating cycle of good intention-failure-guilt, you will not get better on your own. You need the help of other people."[3]

Ask for help from your husband, a girlfriend, or your pastor or women's leader. Your united prayers are a powerful weapon against temptation. And exposing your problem to the light of day is an important step in eliminating it.

Turn Your Weaknesses into Strengths

May I remind you that temptation itself is not a sin? We think of the Devil's attacks as scary or bad or something to be avoided. But it's the *sin* we want to avoid. Temptation can be a positive part of our spiritual growth. We can learn to beat the Devil at his own game.

In 1 Samuel 21, David's enemies were pursuing him, and he had no weapon to defend himself. He asked a priest if there was a sword, spear, or anything he could use. The priest said there was nothing there except the sword of Goliath whom David had killed. The weapon had been wrapped up in a cloth and hidden. David said, "There is none like it; give it to me" (verse 9).

Imagine what a huge sword it was! But David was no longer the young shepherd boy with a sling. He was a grown man and an experienced soldier. His enemy's weapon became his best defense. It can be the same for us. Let me give you an example.

I don't consider myself a grudge-holder. But a few years ago a good friend of mine, whom I'll call Susan, betrayed our ministry and me. I was deeply hurt and angry, and found myself giving in to the temptation to hold on to my bitterness. I realized this was destructive and I wanted to be rid of it, so I determined to obey the Scripture, "Love your enemies and pray for those who persecute you" (Matthew 5:44). I knew it wouldn't be easy to love this woman, but I could certainly pray for her.

Each time I thought of Susan or her name was mentioned, the hurt would rise up in me, followed by a train of negative thoughts. But I allowed these to be a trigger for me to immediately pray for her.

At first my prayers went something like this. *God, deal with Susan. Help her to see how wrong she was. Help her to act like a real Christian.*

What I was really praying was that God would get revenge for me. But I kept on praying for Susan each time I was tempted to feel resentful. And before long I was praying sincere prayers for God's blessing in her life. Eventually, my negative feelings dissipated and I found myself thinking positive thoughts about her and sincerely wishing her well. God showed me how I could use the temptation to help facilitate my healing. What had been intended for evil in my life was turned into something good.

I ran into Susan a few weeks ago. We didn't have much time to talk, but she hugged me enthusiastically and after a little small talk said, "I am so glad we bumped into each other. I've wanted to tell you — you were right about so many things."

In his book *How to Be Born Again*, Billy Graham writes about some prominent men in Scotland who spent the day fishing. That evening as they were having tea in a small inn, one of the fishermen, in the traditional exaggeration of describing the big fish that got away, threw out his hands. He didn't realize the waitress was standing at his side just about to set the tea on the table. His hand knocked the cup out of her hand, sending the tea cup crashing against the wall. The tea spilled all over the white wall, leaving an ugly brown stain. Embarrassed, the man jumped up to help clean it. One of the men at the table said, "Never mind." He pulled out his pen and began to sketch around the brown stain. The result was a picture of a magnificent royal stag with spreading antlers. The artist was Sir Edwin Landseer, England's foremost painter of animals.[4]

To the person who made the mistake, the stain was an embarrassment. But to the artist's eye, it was a thing of beauty. God is the ultimate artist who can turn our stains into works of art.

When you're tempted with jealousy, lust, contention, criticism, or whatever — redirect your thinking and your actions. Do just the opposite of what your carnal self wants to do. You will beat the Devil at his own game, and he'll flee like the coward he is.

Rick Warren suggests we learn from our temptations by recognizing their pattern. We need to ask ourselves, "*When* am I most vulnerable to temptation? *Where* am I usually tempted? *Who* am I with? *How* do I usually feel?" Is it when you're hurt, angry, depressed, or happy? We need to make note of the fertile environment of our temptations and avoid those situations whenever possible.[5]

I hope you used the test at the end of chapter 2 to help determine which personality type you are. When we know our vulnerabilities, we can allow God to develop character and the fruit of the Spirit in our life, in spite of them. When we pray specifically about our negative thoughts or behavior, those temptations become opportunities for God to bring about good in our lives.

LIVE A HOLY LIFE

We've established that we can't live sinless lives on our own. We need the Holy Spirit's help to make the right choices—and we still need God's forgiveness daily. But the Bible is a blueprint for what a Christian life should look like—it is a set of instructions for holy living. Living to please God is not rocket science. It's actually pretty simple, but it does take effort and a sincere desire to please our heavenly Father.

The fruit of the Spirit includes virtues such as love, joy, peace, and long-suffering (Galatians 5:22), all definitely on God's *do* list. Jesus' Sermon on the Mount (Matthew 5) unquestionably gives us a list of God's VIPs—the merciful, the peacemakers, the poor in spirit, the meek, and others. First Corinthians 13, the love chapter, shows us how to love perfectly and how important Christlike love is. Take time to read these passages over and over until they are firmly etched in your mind and heart. From the

Law of Moses in the Old Testament to Jesus' teachings in the Gospels to John's Revelation—the entirety of the Bible makes it clear what God expects from us. This is another good reason to know the Bible.

Micah was a prophet who lived in a very wicked time. One of the kings who ruled during Micah's lifetime was Ahaz, the most ungodly king in Israel's history. In fact, Ahaz even offered his own son to the pagan god Molech. The prophet's teachings might seem basic to you, but his world needed his message. They needed to get back to basics, and Micah told them:

> What doth the Lord require of thee, but to do justly, and to love mercy, and to walk humbly with thy God? (6:8, KJV).

Just like the people in Micah's day, our postmodern society has lost its moral compass. Many Christians live in the gray areas of temptation and compromise. We could all do with a refresher course in the basics of holy living. Here's what Micah instructs us to do.

- Act justly. To act justly means to respect and obey God's law, including the Ten Commandments and other scriptural guidelines for holy living. God is a righteous God and requires us to act fairly and justly to others.

  Do you do what's just in all situations? Are you always honest with your husband? Or do you hide spending through slight adjustments to the checkbook? Do you get your way through manipulation and telling half-truths? Do you treat your children fairly? At work, do you give an honest day's work for your paycheck? Do you cut corners or compromise quality? Do you see wrongs being done, but remain silent? Are you honest, even when no one will know? We need to do what we know is *right*.

- Love mercy. When justice is mentioned in the Bible, many times it's paired with mercy or forgiveness. Justice is the law; mercy is grace. God's character is a perfect blend of justice and mercy. He is holy, but longsuffering and merciful to us.

   Do you give others the benefit of the doubt? Do you withhold punishment when it is deserved? It's not enough to occasionally show mercy, we are told to *love* mercy. It should be the rule rather than the exception. Jesus demonstrated this quality profoundly when He forgave those who were crucifying Him. Revenge and unforgiveness have no place in a holy life. Return good for evil. Treat others like you'd like to be treated. Forgive offenses quickly. It will bring *favor in the sight of God and men* (Proverbs 3:3-4).

- Walk humbly. Humility was as unpopular in Micah's day as it is in our day. The Israelites were arrogant, idolatrous, and proud. Most of Micah's preaching warned about coming destruction, but no one was listening. Because God's holy temple was in Jerusalem, they had a false sense of security.

   Does this not remind you of the United States? We are proud, self-sufficient, and resist being dependent on anyone or anything. This is dangerous for a nation and for us as individuals. We can only please God when we acknowledge our total dependence on Him. That is true humility.

Basics for Holy Living:

- Act justly — Our attitude toward God and His laws
- Love mercy — Our attitude toward others
- Walk humbly — Our attitude toward ourselves

So let's get back to basics. It is possible for us to be holy and please God with our lives. We will never be perfect, but with the help of the Holy Spirit, we can defeat temptation and grow in righteousness and obedience. "For God is at work within you, helping you want to obey him, and then helping you do what he wants" (Philippians 2:13, TLB).

DEVELOP A HOLY HATRED FOR SIN

A pastor friend of mine, Colin Smith, preaches a sermon called "Learning How to Hate." It's an odd message from a preacher to a congregation of Christians who are taught from infancy they should *love* one another. But if we *love* deeply, then we will *hate* deeply the things that threaten what we love. I grew up to hate alcohol because I saw what it did to some members of my family. Cancer has ravaged those we love, so we hate the disease. Pastor Smith says we must develop a "holy hatred for sin."[6]

If we truly love God, we must learn to hate that which separates us from fellowship with Him. One reason we keep yielding to the same temptations over and over is because we don't hate the sin. Oh, we may be sorry. But the offense is not so detestable to us that we turn away from it forever.

How do we develop holy hatred for sin? A young missionary couple who worked in the most decadent part of Amsterdam said, "Whenever we can look at the sin all around us and not be horrified, we go away for two weeks of prayer and fasting." Perhaps all of us need to renew our horror of sin through prayer and fasting.

We can also come to hate sin by looking around and seeing what sin has done to our loved ones, including Jesus. Mel Gibson's film *The Passion of the Christ* was used in miraculous ways all around the world. But the most poignant message for me was to see what my sin had done to Jesus. It wasn't the Jews or the Romans who crucified Jesus. It was my sin. And it was your sin.

Are you tolerating sin in your life? Picture the unthinkable agony of the Cross. When we turn a deaf ear to the Holy Spirit's warning that we are about to step over the line, we put our hand atop the soldier's as he lays open the Lord's back with the cat-of-nine-tails. When we hold onto that one "small" sin that no one else knows about, we help to drive the spikes through Jesus' hands and feet. God knew our weakness and that we would never be able to overcome sin. So the only way we could be spared was for His Son to die. Our sinfulness made the Cross necessary. I pray our blinders be removed and that we develop a holy hatred for sin that will help us keep it out of our lives.

Grow Your Relationship with Jesus

Love changes things—radically. My friend and cohost Michelle McKinney Hammond says:

> Love will make you do right even when you want to do wrong. Love will make you change everything from your personality to the color of your hair. Love makes people do some strange things. And that's the stuff we do when we are in love with a human being. . . . How much more should our love for God keep us from falling prey to the flirtations of Temptations?[7]

Yes, love *will* cause us to do right when we want to do wrong. The most important weapon to overcoming temptation is an intense, intimate relationship with Jesus Christ—a thriving, passionate, all-encompassing love connection that filters our every decision and every action.

Initially, our love affair with Jesus is usually intense. But as time goes by, we begin to take our relationship and His love for granted. All love relationships have highs and lows, days when the emotion and outward manifestations of our affection wane and recede. If we don't work at it, the spark of love will grow cold and even go out completely. When our love for God loses its intensity, we become vulnerable to temptation.

When I was dating, like most young people I was often tempted to go "all the way," as we called it back in the sixties. But I never did. And while the fear of pregnancy, fear of my parents' wrath, and my personal moral boundaries were strong deterrents, the thing that really kept me pure was my love for Jesus. I stopped short of committing that sin because I felt so close to Him I just couldn't stand the thought of hurting Him that way.

If that sounds a bit super-spiritual, I assure you I have failed and disappointed Jesus many, many times, despite my love for Him. All of us do. But if you find yourself yielding to temptation too often, it's time to fall in love again.

You may be asking yourself, "How can I love God more?" One way is to better understand how much He loves *you*. A woman often falls in love with the man she ultimately marries because *he* first got interested in *her*. She may not have been at all attracted at first, but his love eventually drew her in. When you focus on God's love for you, you cannot help but love Him in return. Study His many promises to you in the Bible. Read the Psalms every day. Ask Him to reveal Himself to you so that your love can grow.

THE SECRET PLACE

Keep in mind that love takes commitment, sacrifice—and considerable chunks of time. It can be a struggle to spend quality time with the Lord in personal devotions, quiet time, meditation, and Bible study, even when we are not busy and have the time to spend with Him.

Many years ago I had to undergo abdominal surgery for a femoral hernia. It was an emergency situation, but not a serious operation. However, I had to be careful about my activity for several weeks after the surgery. I couldn't do any heavy work, lifting, or straining—even things like closing a window.

Prior to the surgery I looked forward to this time of recuperation. I thought I would have some uninterrupted time to spend in prayer, Bible reading, and personal worship. I made arrangements for the children, rides to school, meals for the next week or so, and cleared my calendar.

But I made a surprising discovery. Although I did have more free time after the surgery, it was just as much a struggle to spend quality time with the Lord as it had ever been. I had always blamed the demands of my life and my busyness for my haphazard and inconsistent personal devotions. But every time I would open my Bible or bow my head to pray, something would distract me. The phone would ring, or I would suddenly become very sleepy or hungry. Maybe it was the after-effects of the anesthetic, but I found it difficult to focus on prayer or the Bible.

God showed me that although I desired to spend meaningful time with Him, it would always be a struggle. Building intimacy with God begins with a decision and continues through determination and discipline. Prayer is hard work. Labor. But it yields huge dividends and is the very best defense against temptation.

A few years ago I read a book that revolutionized my personal time with the Lord: *Secrets of the Secret Place* by Bob Sorge. The book begins with a story about Chris and DeeAnn, a young couple who faced a huge financial crisis. They decided to spend some time praying together about the situation. As they prayed, they heard an audible voice say "If you need help call 9-1-1."

LEARN TO HATE, FALL IN LOVE, AND WIN

The voice repeated this message four or five times. Thinking it was coming from the garage, they slowly opened the door and looked inside. Everything seemed in perfect order, except in the center of the floor lay a toy ambulance. Chris picked it up and pushed a button next to the emergency lights. "If you need help call 9-1-1." As they stood wondering how in the world this mechanism could have activated itself, Chris felt the Holy Spirit say, "If you need help call 9-1-1 — Psalms 91:1."

Chris and DeeAnn returned to their family room and read the verse together: "He who dwells in the secret place of the Most High shall abide under the shadow of the Almighty." The couple knew God was telling them to renew their commitment to the secret place of relationship with Him. They understood God would direct them in their financial decisions as they gave themselves to the intimacy of abiding in the presence of the Almighty.[8]

How many of our problems would shrink into perspective if only we would focus on the secret place? There, our spirits become more sensitive to God's voice and we become more intolerant of our own sin.

Your intimate time with God should not be a distasteful chore. God despises meaningless rituals and religious posturing. He loves genuine worship. Though prayer is hard work and the secret place takes discipline, therein lies the greatest blessing of our Christian experience. Bob paints this serene and beautiful picture of what our private time with God should look like:

One of the best kept secrets of our faith is the blessedness and joy of cultivating a secret life with God. Imagine . . . you're tucked away in a quiet nook; the door is shut; you're curled up in a comfortable position; the living word of God is laid open before you; Jesus himself stands at your side . . . your love is awakened . . . your spirit is ignited and your mind is renewed; you talk to him and he talks to you in the language of intimate friendship.[9]

This is the real beauty of the secret place—deep communion with God and true worship. But our lifestyles and mindset are in direct opposition to it. In order to enter into God's presence, we must get alone, close the door, quiet our bodies and our spirits, and *listen*, as well as pray. It's not something we do naturally or easily. But we must cultivate the riches of the secret place, or we will never win over temptation.

I challenge you to try it. Read *Secrets of the Secret Place* and other books that can help you enrich and maximize your personal devotions. It doesn't matter if you have your quiet time in the morning or in the evening or, as Bob suggests, both. If you miss a day or two, don't be riddled with guilt and slink away in shame. Keep coming back.

Of course, we can pray at work or in the car or when we exercise. We can become so close to our heavenly Father that our prayers flow as easily as breathing anytime, anyplace. I want to live continuously in His presence. But nothing is a fitting substitute for the secret place. Return to your sanctuary with the eagerness of a starving woman to a banquet table, knowing that the One who loves you will be waiting.

Say "yes" to the secret place. Pain is healed there. Ministries are born there. Creativity explodes there. And under the shadow of the Almighty you will begin to take on the characteristics of your heavenly Father. It is there you can win your victory over temptation—and break the curse of The Eve Factor.

CHAPTER NINE:
LEARN TO HATE, FALL IN LOVE, AND WIN

Study and Explore

Read the following verses and write down the ways they give for overcoming temptation.

Example: Psalms 91:1—By spending time in the secret place
Matthew 6:14-15
Romans 16:20
1 Corinthians 10:13
2 Corinthians 10:3-5
Ephesians 6:13-18
1 John 1:9
1 John 5:4-5

Consider and Reflect

1. What are the first two critical steps in overcoming temptation?

2. How can we use our temptations to grow stronger?

3. What are three commands the prophet Micah gives for living a holy life?

4. Write out your own definitions for justice, mercy, and humility.

5. Why is having an accountability partner so important in overcoming temptation?

6. As you have read this book, has the Holy Spirit showed you areas of failure? Make a list of the temptations most prevalent in your life.

7. Think of the times you have yielded to temptation and ultimately sinned. Have you confessed those to God and asked for forgiveness? It is never too late to make things right.

8. Do you hate the sin in your life or do you tolerate it? Take a moment to reflect on what your sin cost God's Son.

9. Can you think of at least one occasion when you turned a temptation around to bring spiritual growth? Explain how you did it.

10. Have there been times when your love for Christ was more intense than it is today? Think of ways you can rekindle that love.

11. Which of the following holds you back from spending quality time with the Lord?

   - Busy schedule
   - Small children
   - Distractions and interruptions
   - Lack of desire
   - Lack of self-discipline
   - Lack of energy
   - Sabotage by the Enemy
   - Other _____

Talk to the Lord about each obstacle to the secret place and ask for His help in developing intimacy with Him and the spiritual strength to overcome temptation.

Pray

Dear Jesus, I confess my temptation and sin. Thank You for showing me my areas of weakness and failure. Give me a sensitive spirit and a listening ear to Your ongoing correction and conviction when I make mistakes. Give me the desire to live a holy life and the strength to resist temptation. Help me to defeat the Enemy and my own fleshly nature. Help me to be accountable to my husband or others so there will be no secret temptations or sins in my life. Help me to keep growing toward the intimate relationship You intended for us. Help me to become more and more like my Father. In Your name, Amen.

NOTES

Chapter 1
1. *Oxford American Dictionary* (New York: Avon Books, 1980), 706.
2. Bob Sorge, *Secrets of the Secret Place* (Greenwood, MO: Oasis House, 2001), 20-21.

Chapter 2
1. Florence Littauer, *Personality Plus* (Grand Rapids, MI: Revell, 1983, 1992), 11.
2. Littauer, 36.
3. Littauer, 111.
4. Littauer, 61.
5. Littauer, 142, 144.

Chapter 3
1. Mary Ellen Ashcroft, *Temptations Women Face* (Downers Grove, IL: InterVarsity, 1991), 144.
2. Carolyn Heilbrun, As quoted by Ashcroft, 29.
3. Jurgen Moltman, As quoted by Ashcroft, 29-30.
4. Linda T. Stanford and Mary Ellen Donovan, As quoted by Ashcroft, 30.
5. Stanford and Donovan, As quoted by Ashcroft.

Chapter 4
1. Rick Ezell, *The 7 Sins of Highly Defective People* (Grand Rapids, MI: Kregel, 2003), 70.
2. Charles Swindoll, *The Tale of the Tardy Oxcart and 1501 Other Stories* (Nashville, TN, 1998), 114. (Swindoll footnotes it as from a book or article by Tozer titled, "The Root of Righteousness.")
3. Jerry Rose, *Deep Faith for Dark Valleys* (Nashville, TN: Thomas Nelson, 2003), 32-38.
4. James M. Freeman, *Manners and Customs of the Bible* (Logos International, 1972), 204.

Chapter 5
1. Beth Moore, *Praying God's Word* (Nashville, TN: Broadman and Holman, 2000), 3-4.
2. *Oxford American Dictionary* (New York: Avon Books, 1980), 803.
3. Kayanne Janiga, MSN, RN, is a nurse and therapist who has worked with individuals, children, and families in a variety of pediatric and psychiatric

environments. She has served as professor of nursing and a curriculum and program writer, founder, and developer.
4. Janiga, MSN, RN.
5. Oswald Chambers, *My Utmost for His Highest* (Discovery House, 1989).
6. Chambers, *Prayer: A Holy Occupation*, edited by Harry Verploegh (Grand Rapids, MI: Discovery House, 1992), 119.
7. Chambers, *The Shadow of an Agony* (Discovery House, 1992).

Chapter 6

1. Barna Research Group, *Beliefs: General Religious*, "Percentage of Adults Who View Certain Behavior as Morally Acceptable" (2003).
2. Jayne Schooler, "Mom, I'm Pregnant and I Want an Abortion," *Right to the Heart* Ezine, RighttoTheHeart@aol.com, September 2004.
3. Catherine Hickem as quoted by Schooler.
4. Karen Mains, *The God Hunt* (Downers Grove, IL: Intervarsity, 2003).

Chapter 7

1. C. S. Lewis, *The Screwtape Letters* (New York, NY: MacMillan), 17.
2. Rick Ezell, *The 7 Sins of Highly Defective People* (Kregel, 2003), 25.
3. Mary Ellen Ashcroft, *Temptations Women Face* (Downers Grove, IL: InterVarsity, 1991), 104-105.
4. Ashcroft, 105.

Chapter 8

1. Supplement, *Total Living Drink*, can be ordered from Kylea Health and Energy on www.kylea.com.
2. Rick Warren, *The Purpose-Driven Life* (Grand Rapids, MI: Zondervan, 2002), 31.

Chapter 9

1. Rick Warren, *The Purpose-Driven Life* (Grand Rapids, MI: Zondervan, 2002), 204.
2. Bob Sorge, *Secrets of the Secret Place* (Greenwood, MO: Oasis House, 2001), 95.
3. Warren, 212.
4. Billy Graham, *How to Be Born Again* (Waco, TX: Word, 1977), 129-130.
5. Warren, 206.
6. Colin Smith, Tape Series *The Secret Life of the Soul*, "Learning How to Hate," 2002.
7. Michelle McKinney Hammond, *Why Do I Say Yes When I Need to Say No?* (Eugene, OR: Harvest House, 2002), 175.
8. Sorge, 3-4.
9. Sorge, 4.

ABOUT THE AUTHOR

For over twenty-five years Shirley has demonstrated, through her books, the television show she created, and her teaching, her passion for God and for helping women grow. Shirley's speaking and Bible studies have touched women from as far away as Australia, from drug-addicted pregnant women of the inner city to the most affluent of Chicago's Gold Coast.

She is a mother of three grown children and the grandmother of six. Drawing from a rich background of corporate business, paired with ministry and the personal challenges of raising her own children, Shirley's experience and spiritual sensitivity can touch women in all phases of life.

As executive producer and cohost of *Aspiring Women*, Shirley has developed an award-winning television program that meets women where they are. It features true stories from across the country that address candidly and effectively the challenging issues women face. The Emmy-nominated program is syndicated across the U.S. and in more than thirty countries overseas.

She is a member of Advanced Writers and Speakers Association, Women in Christian Media, and the National Academy of Television Arts and Sciences, and serves as a presenter at the annual Emmy Awards. She works at the Total Living Network (TLN) where her husband Jerry is President and CEO. In addition to his duties at TLN, Jerry serves as associate pastor of a small Baptist church.

If your church or women's ministry is interested in scheduling Shirley for a conference, retreat, banquet, or training event, please contact:

Total Living Network
2880 Vision Court
Aurora, Il 60506
630-801-3679
srose@tln.com

SHAPE YOUR LIFE FROM THE INSIDE OUT.

Secret Longings of the Heart
Carol Kent
1-57683-360-7

Here is a rich encounter with the hidden desires of women today—
the passions that determine lifestyle, behavior, and attitudes—and
how these relate to serving and loving God.

Finding Calm in Life's Chaos
Becky Harling
1-57683-619-3

Finding Calm in Life's Chaos connects women's emotional needs
with Jesus' "I am" statements, helping readers find peace, comfort,
and security in the character and presence of God.

Growing by Heart
Scharlotte Rich
1-57683-683-5

Beautifully designed, this garden-themed devotional encourages
women and teaches them how to memorize Scripture. It contains
over one hundred different pullout memory cards, each one
featuring a small floral design.